The Economics of Globalization and Artificial Intelligence

Nicola Acocella

The Economics of Globalization and Artificial Intelligence

Utilizing AI for the Benefit of Humanity

palgrave
macmillan

Nicola Acocella
Sapienza University of Rome
Rome, Italy

ISBN 978-3-032-15710-2 ISBN 978-3-032-15711-9 (eBook)
https://doi.org/10.1007/978-3-032-15711-9

This Palgrave Macmillan imprint is published by the registered company Springer Nature Switzerland AG.
The registered company address is: Gewerbestrasse 11, 6330 Cham, Switzerland

Contents

List of Figures

List of Tables

CHAPTER 1

Introduction

Abstract Globalization is an intensification of the global interconnectedness that manifests itself in the form of movements of people (and of communications and ideas), goods and services, and capital.

AI is the branch of computer science dedicated to creating machines that are able to think like humans. It's about taking the unique abilities of the human brain to understand, react, and interpret and incorporating those abilities into computers and other devices.

Different phases of globalization have been devised.

The three following characteristics can define AI:

1. Intentionality, which means that the AI system takes intentional decisions, rather than merely being programmed with predetermined responses.
2. Use of intelligence, often coming from interaction with machine learning and data analytics programs.
3. Adaptability, which means that AI systems adjust as they receive new data, make decisions, and interpret the outcomes.

Keywords Globalization • Artificial Intelligence • Movements of people • Movement of goods and services • Movement of capital • Phases of globalization • Characteristics of globalization

N. Acocella, *The Economics of Globalization and Artificial Intelligence*, https://doi.org/10.1007/978-3-032-15711-9_1

Let us first briefly define globalization and Artificial Intelligence (AI). Globalization is an intensification of global interconnectedness (Held et al., 1999) that manifests itself in the form of movements of people (and of communications and ideas), goods and services, and capital. People live now in an interconnected world, but the phenomenon of globalization has a long history, which also correlates to climate change, trade wars, and fears of nuclear conflicts.

In the simplest of terms, AI is the branch of computer science dedicated to creating machines that are able to think like humans. It's about taking the unique abilities of the human brain to understand, react, and interpret, and incorporating those abilities into computers and other devices. AI seems to be quite a complicated field, but it essentially boils down to two key components: data and algorithms. Vast amounts of data are used in conjunction with algorithms to essentially 'train' AI to be able to learn and grow of its own accord, without the need for programming and code updates.

The idea of AI has been around for a long time. But, for many decades, it was reserved for the realms of science fiction. However, the work of Alan Turing in the 1950s and many other great minds that followed gradually led to the rise of machine learning and the development of genuine AI solutions.

This all culminated with the so-called 'AI boom' that became most prominent in 2022, as large language models (LLMs) and AI chatbots, like ChatGPT, were released for public usage. Since then, AI has taken off, with many businesses embracing the tech in exciting, innovative ways.

AI is the computer science field creating machines that mimic human intelligence and use algorithms to simulate human-like behavior and decision-making. AI has extended its innovative embrace to a wide range of sectors, beyond exports, and has transformed them radically. In the field of healthcare, AI has revolutionized medical diagnosis, thanks to advanced imaging systems that analyze radiological images and scans to detect pathologies with a precision that was unthinkable until a few years ago. In addition, pharmaceutical research is using AI to accelerate the development of new drugs. AI has also become a powerful weapon for data analysis and financial market forecasting. Finally, AI is revolutionizing the education sector, through the personalization of learning through intelligent tutoring systems. Like economic globalization, AI developments promise benefits, including job creation and price reduction, but also costs, such as job losses, raising crucial questions about public perception (Magistro et al., 2025).

Definition and Manifestations of Globalization

One of the earliest and most influential definitions of globalization came from sociologist Roland Robertson, who described it as 'the compression of the world and the intensification of consciousness of the world as a whole.' This definition highlights two important aspects of globalization: the shrinking of space and time due to technological advances, and the growing awareness of global interconnectedness among people worldwide. For Robertson, globalization is not just about the physical movement of goods or people, but also about how individuals and societies come to understand themselves in relation to the global context.

Another influential perspective on globalization comes from sociologist Anthony Giddens, who defines it as 'the intensification of worldwide social relations which link distant localities in such a way that local happenings are shaped by events occurring many miles away and vice versa' (Sociology Institute, sociology-of-development, 2023).

The term globalization as integration of the world's economies, politics, and cultures seems to have been coined in a 1983 article titled 'The Globalization of Markets' by the German-American economist Theodore Levitt.

According to the Britannica Encyclopedia the central aspects of globalization are 'interconnection, intensification, time-space distanciation (conditions that allow time and space to be organised in a manner that connects presence and absence), supraterritoriality, time-space compression, action at a distance, and accelerating interdependence. Modern analysts also conceive globalisation as a long-term process of deterritorialization of social activities (economic, political, and cultural) occurring without regard for geographic location. Thus, globalisation can be defined as the stretching of economic, political, and social relationships in space and time. A manufacturer assembling a product for a distant market, a country submitting to international law, and a language adopting a foreign loanword are all examples of globalisation.' International movements of people are of short or long duration. The former are in particular for tourism or short stays for work or care. The latter correspond to international migration, which is to add to migration within a country. Obviously, these flows may involve people with more or less professional training and may have different basic motivations, ranging from political (often corresponding to persecutions, wars, or the like) or health (epidemics) or economic reasons such as search for work and livelihood. Both in the past and now all these reasons have been or are widely present.

The globalization of the movement of goods and services corresponds to the worldwide extension of trade in goods. This can be the exchange of raw materials, semi-finished products, final products or their component parts, or exchanges of services, such as the rental or insurance of goods, financial intermediation services, information-technology (IT) services (e.g., for processing data) and communication,[1] royalties and licenses for the exploitation of patents and similar, copyright and image rights.

International capital movements are of various types. In fact, there are movements of financial capital under the form of loans at different maturities, short, medium, or long. Short-term capital movements often have a high speculative component, which can lead to high returns (or losses), connected in particular with changes in exchange rates. For example, those who expect the dollar to appreciate in the short term against the euro will buy short-term dollar-denominated loans or securities, to sell them once the dollar has appreciated. Medium- and long-term capital movements that tend to exploit the higher yields of securities issued abroad are intended to be held for a certain time and are therefore called portfolio investments. They include purchases of shares to an extent that does not give rise to control of the companies that issue them. Instead, the capital movements that lead to the acquisition of controlling interests in pre-existing or newly founded foreign companies are foreign direct investments (FDIs). These companies, which usually have subsidiaries in various countries, are called multinationals or multinational companies or transnational corporations (TNCs). These companies have played an increasing role in economic, financial, human, and cultural flows.

Understanding globalization requires recognizing that it's not just an economic or political phenomenon, but also a social and cultural one that shapes the way we live, interact, and view the world.

One of the most profound impacts of globalization is on culture. Globalization has led to the diffusion of cultural products—such as music, movies, fashion, and food—across the world. Popular culture, especially from the United States, has spread globally, influencing fashion trends, music, and entertainment preferences. Think of how movies like 'The Avengers' or TV shows like 'Friends' are watched around the world, creating a shared cultural experience across national boundaries.

[1] The growth of communications and the circulation of information should be considered as an addition to (and within certain limits a substitute for) the physical movements of people, constituting their *virtual* movement.

However, the spread of cultural products is not a one-way process. While Western culture has a significant influence globally, other cultures have also made their mark. For instance, the popularity of yoga, Bollywood films, or even the global fascination with K-pop (Korean pop music) highlights the growing influence of non-Western cultures in global cultural exchanges. Globalization, in this sense, is not only about the dominance of one culture but also about the interplay and mixing of different cultural elements.

This cultural exchange can result in what some scholars refer to as 'glocalisation,' a term that describes the blending of global and local cultures. As people in different parts of the world adopt and adapt global cultural products, they often re-interpret these elements in ways that align with their local customs and traditions. For example, the global spread of fast food chains like McDonald's has led to the creation of localized versions of the menu, such as the 'Paneer Maharaja Mac' in India (Sociology Institute, sociology-of-development, 2023).

A more detailed picture of information about the forms of globalization with reference to the period after 1850 and up to the beginning of the current century is offered in Table 1.1 below.

Different phases of globalization have been devised. According to some economists, globalization first started with the discovery of the Americas by Christopher Columbus. There was certainly a movement of people between the continents, which also increased trade, but the numbers of the world trade did not increase too much (only 1% per year from 1500 to 1800). The term 'the first globalisation' has been introduced to describe the world's first major period of globalization of trade and finance, which took place between 1850 or 1870 and 1914. The 'second globalisation,' instead, began in 1944—after a period of wars and economic crises—and ended in 1971.[2] This led to the third era of globalization, one characterized by the lack of a single leading nation or foundational project, begun in 1989—with the dismantling of the Soviet Union and the rise of a multipolar world—and ended around the early 2020s.

Table 1.1 indicates the main aspects of these three eras.

The development of communication and transportation and adoption of laissez-faire policies by many countries allowed the first phase of globalization to develop. Integration during the first globalization period took

[2] On the evolution of world trade, 1870–1949, one can usefully see Klasing and Milionis (2014).

Table 1.1 Main aspects of the first three globalization phases

Time period	*1860–1914*	*1944–1971*	*1989–*
Technology	Steam engine	Jet planes	Microprocessor
	Telegraph	Television	PC
	Electricity	Communication satellites	Internet
	Internal combustion engine	Container traffic	Mobile telephones
Political leadership	Great Britain economic leader	USA economic leader	Multi-polar (USA, EU, China)
	Colonialism	Cold War	Global democratic processes
Commerce	Initially free trade, but increasing protectionism	Gradually reduced industrial tariffs	More and more countries adopt free trade
Trade in services	Limited scale	Limited scale	Increased scale in more and more branches
	Shipping industry most important	Shipping industry most important	
Capital movement	Free	Regulated	Free
Migration	Free movement	Regulated (excluding Nordic countries)	Regulated (excluding EU)
	Emigration	Labor migration	Political migration

Source: Nordregio (n.d.)

place in terms of the ratio of commodity trade to GDP and the cost of moving goods or factors of production across borders. In addition, the international price gaps fell. For example, 'the price gap of wheat between Liverpool and Chicago fell from 57,6% to 15,6%, and the price gap of bacon between London and Cincinnati fell from 92,5% to 17,9%' (Wikipedia). Migration had an important role for the first globalization, as the number of transoceanic migrants and those coming to European countries was very high due to the higher wages earned and the very opportunity to find a job. The fact that American and Australian workers earned higher wages than their European counterparts was the main reason for the mass migrations. In Europe workers' living standard rose as migration to America lowered the labor supply and pushed up real wages.[3]

[3] Table 1.3 reports many data about the main indicators of globalization in the nineteenth, twentieth, and twenty-first centuries.

Many factors contributed to the growth of international trade. These were mainly: falling transportation costs, reduction of trade barriers and move to free trade in several countries. 'Europe was a net exporter of manufactures and a net importer of primary products. The New World exchanged food and raw materials for European manufactured goods. This ended up being beneficial for European workers because, in the era where a large portion of income was still spent on food, cheaper transport meant cheaper food and thus higher real wages. However, it was not so beneficial for farmers. Only in countries that retained agricultural free trade, like the United Kingdom, were less vulnerable to the price and rent reductions that globalization implied. Trade between industrialized economies was the prevalent form of trade before 1914' (Daudin et al., 2008).

Table 1.2 shows the four stages of globalization, starting from the beginning of the last century. It indicates, in addition to the time span of each stage, the leading exports and nations, the corresponding main

Table 1.2 Globalization eras and their enabling innovations

Globalization-era/ stage	*Leading exports*	*Leading nations*	*Enabling tech-no-era for globalization era*	*Enabling innovations*	*Titans of globalization era*
Globalization 1.0 / 1900–1914	Textile, industrial goods	Great Britain	1st Industrial Revolution (1780s–middle of nineteenth century)	Steam engine, steam trains and ships	Railroad companies
Globalization 2.0 / 1945–1989	Factories	US, USSR	2nd Industrial Revolution (1870s–1910s)	Assembly line, automobile, airplane	Ford, Exxon Mobil, GM
Globalization 3.0 / 1989–2008	Global supply chains	US	3rd Industrial Revolution (1960s–1990s)	Computer, Internet	IBM, HP, Dell, Microsoft
Globalization 4.0/ 2008+ Digital Globalization 2014+	Digital goods/ services /// data, information	US, China	4th Industrial Revolution (2000–2010s)	Robotization, Artificial Intelligence, autonomous vehicles, Internet of Things	Google (Alphabet), Facebook, Amazon, Tencent

Source: Alyoshina (2019)

Table 1.3 Indicators of globalization in the nineteenth, twentieth, and twenty-first centuries

World	*1850–1913*	*1914–1949*	*1950–1973*	*1974–2007*
Growth of population	0.8	1.7	1.9	1.6
Growth of GDP (real)	2.1	3.8	5.1	2.9
Growth of per capita GDP	1.3	2.0	3.1	1.2
Growth of commerce (real)	3.8	6.2	8.2	5.0
Migration (net cumulative) to the United States, Canada, Australia, NZ				
Millions	17.9	50.1	12.7	37.4
Growth of population 2007–2023: 1.16%				
Growth of GDP 2007–2023: 2.6				
Growth of per capita GDP 2007–2023: 1.50				
Growth of exports 2007–2023: 3.0%				
Yearly growth of population, 2007–2023: 0.0112941				

% changes, unless otherwise indicated

Source: World Trade Organization (2008)

instrumental innovation and the leading companies of each. Digital globalization and AI are the main enabling innovations of the contemporary stage of globalization.

For the trend of the world's population growth in the last two to three centuries, see Fig. 1.2. After reaching a maximum of 10.43 billion inhabitants in 2086, there will be a decline. In fact, the rate of growth of the world population has in fact already declined since 1963 and will be −0.1 in 2100.

The period of the 1930s saw a setback for globalization, due to the effects of the Great Crisis that had begun in 1929 and to the prevalence of nationalistic and autarchic attitudes. The setback of trade, investment, and migration can clearly be seen in Fig. 1.1.

Figure 1.2 gives births and deaths since 1950 to 2023 and projections to 2100.

Global merchandise trade and immigration moved largely in parallel 'in the decades leading up to World War I, collapsed during the interwar period, and then rebounded after WWII (but with much more pronounced growth in trade than in immigration for a long period after WWII)' (Jacks & Tang, 2018).

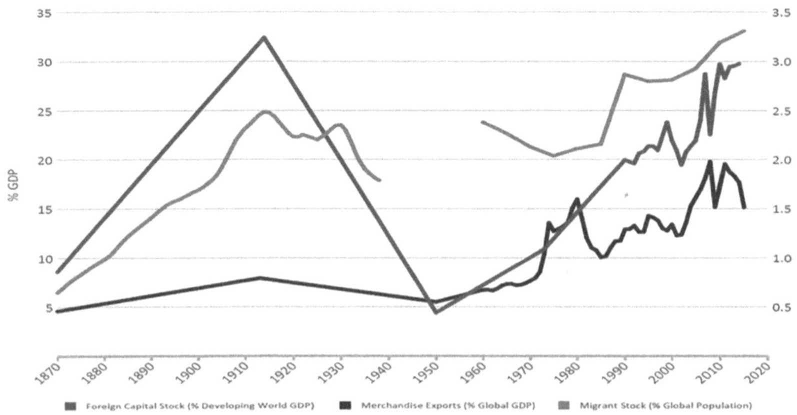

Fig. 1.1 Trends in globalization, 1870–2015. (*Source:* Chandy & Seidel, 2016). *Note:* The broken curve with the largest variations indicates the stock of foreign capital (expressed as a % of the *GDP of developing countries*). The curve that rises smoothly and shows cyclical variations since 1970 indicates exports of goods as a % of *world GDP*. Finally, the curve that breaks between 1940 and 1950 indicates the stock of emigrants as a % of the *world population*

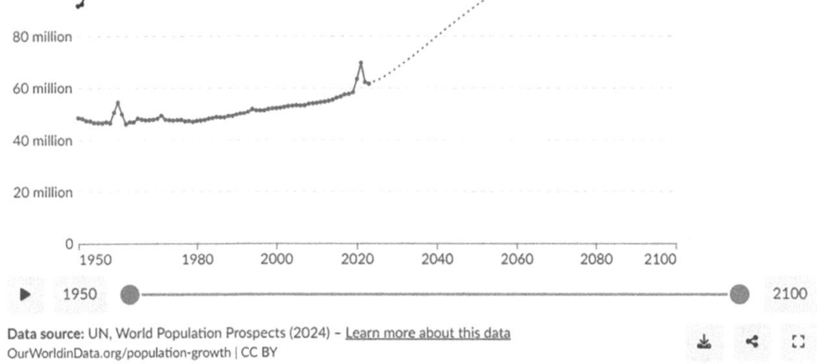

Fig. 1.2 Births and deaths per year, world. (*Source:* UN, World Population Prospects, 2024). *Note:* Projections are based on the UN's medium scenario

The international integration that took place before the Great War could only have specific and limited effects, finding a broad foundation and discipline in the colonial relationship. On the other hand, the number of countries that are part of the global market today is considerably higher than that of pre-1914, although many are still in a marginal position.

Therefore, if even the international economic integration that took place after World War II represents the re-emergence of a trend that characterized the world economy more than a century ago, the resumption of that trend takes place with at least partially new characteristics, which justify the use of the term 'second globalisation,' the first reflecting the integration process prior to the Great War.

As to the inspiratory principles of globalization, liberalism was certainly the guiding principle of the solutions adopted at the international level at the time. It can be found in the liberalization of trade in goods and in the multilateral approach mentioned above. However, as mentioned, it is a principle tempered by Keynesian thought, which grafted onto this liberal basis a series of public intervention policies, mainly aimed at ensuring the maintenance of full employment and the coordination of economic policies. This was behind the symmetry required in the balance of payments rebalancing policies, established with reference to both deficit and surplus countries: the deflationary policies adopted in the former to reduce the deficit itself would have been less burdensome if opposite, expansionary policies had been adopted in the surplus countries.

For the same reason, the liberalization of capital movements was subject to limitations, as will be seen better later. In fact, it could have translated into a further reason for asymmetry, difficult to cure. Furthermore, similar arguments could actually be applied not only to international financial markets, but also—more generally—to all short-term financial markets.

For them, first of all, Keynes's criticism applies that speculation acts like a beauty contest in which the winner is not the one who points out the most beautiful faces, but the one who manages to better understand the prevailing preferences of the participants in the contest by thinking about their idea of beauty about the face itself. Obviously, as has been said, higher-order reasoning of the type 'everyone thinks that the others think, etc.' is likely. More recently, the enormous size of international capital movements (compared to the limited currency reserves available in the various countries and the financing that can be activated with multilateral organizations), the high speed of movements, the manifestation of 'herd' effects—which repeat and amplify the mechanisms at work in the beauty contest—increase the probability of self-fulfilling expectations, having little or no relation to the trend of fundamentals.

As for historical precedents, it must be said that the comparison between the results in terms of growth of both GDP and international trade obtained in the period of the first globalization and the effects of the protectionist policies adopted in the period between the two world wars was valuable. While these policies had greatly limited the growth of international trade, the liberalization preceding the Great War had been a harbinger of growth in trade.

In the past decades globalization has fostered economic growth and cultural exchange, even if it has also exposed economies to the fluctuations in global market; a wide set of potential risks and implications, such as the spread of diseases, posing risks to public health and national security, and additional environmental risks, which have amplified due to global industrialization, and risks deriving from the vast amounts of cross-border data flow, which is vulnerable to hacking, manipulation, and espionage.

Factors in favor of globalization are as follows: formation of a larger market for goods and services; cheaper consumer prices; outsourcing benefitting domestic firms and foreign labor; increased standard of living. Negative consequences of globalization are: concentration of wealth in richer countries; some poorer countries can be left behind; labor and the physical and intellectual resources of poorer countries can be exploited; regions and cultures lose their uniqueness and products available around the world can become homogeneous.

Definitions and Types of AI

'In AI, machines perform tasks like speech recognition, problem-solving, learning, etc. Machines can work and act like a human if they have enough information.' Then, in AI, knowledge engineering plays a vital role by establishing the relationship between objects and their properties (Pedamkar, 2023).

As said by West (2018) and also reported by Global Transactions (2020), the following three characteristics can define AI:

1. Intentionality, which means that the AI system takes intentional decisions, rather than merely being programmed with predetermined responses. This requires AI to understand the meaning of a

query and parse data with the intent to determine the answer, by combining data from different sources, analyzing them immediately, and acting on the conclusions it draws.
2. Use of intelligence, often coming from interaction with machine learning and data analytics programs. 'The combination of these technologies enables what we think of as intelligent decision making. For example, an AI system that assigns students to different school systems cannot rely on rote computations—it must also weigh values such as equity and justice to create beneficial outcomes for all.'
3. Adaptability, which means that 'AI systems adjust as they receive new data, make decisions, and interpret the outcomes. If financial or environmental conditions change—or, in the case of self-driving cars, if road conditions deteriorate—AI can take the new data into account and adjust its decision making accordingly.'

Wodecki (2019) notes that AI covers an interdisciplinary field, integrating notions of logic, mathematics, computer science, psychology and, more recently, management and ethics. It can be developed dynamically as a method and from a technological point of view. It raises many hopes and many fears and controversies (see, e.g., Bostrom, 2014).

In the last 60 years, AI comes after at least four digital revolutions: the advent and proliferation of personal computers; the expansion of the internet; the rise and influence of social media; and the growing mobile computing and connectivity.

AI may create technology-based industries, leading to radical changes in the inputs and outputs of the global economy in the production of goods and services, raise productivity growth and transform lives across the world. The so-called 'AI revolution' sooner or later may happen and countries developing AI capabilities will benefit from it in the future.

AI is essential to Industry 5.0[4] as it offers process optimization, innovation, and human-machine collaboration. 'It supports sustainability activities and improves productivity and efficiency by facilitating smooth communication and decision-making. Robotic systems can now adapt to

[4] This is the fifth industrial revolution, overcoming the limitations of industry 4.0 in terms of production, and aiming to integrate human capabilities into the pre-existing technological production environment. Industry 4.0 made use of processes of digitalization and technological advance by means of automation.

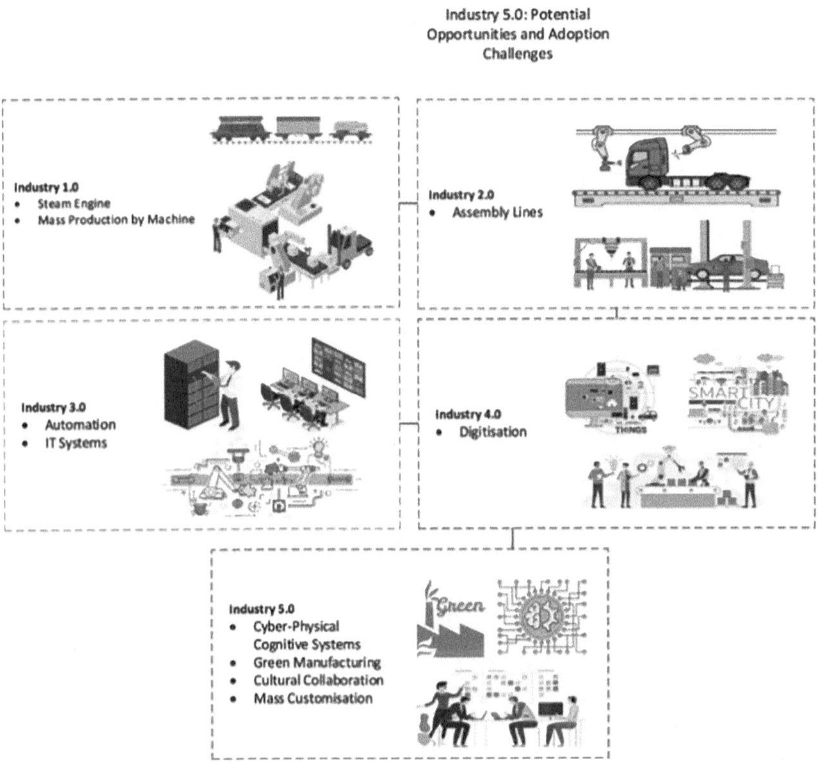

Fig. 1.3 The five stages in the evolution of industry (*Source:* Adel, 2022)

changing manufacturing settings and learn from interactions with human operators thanks to AI-driven technologies like machine learning and data analytics' (Ibrahim et al., 2025).

The five stages in the evolution of industry are shown in Fig. 1.3.

AI can enhance productivity growth, but a host of factors—essentially, waves of complementary innovations and the ability of policymakers and firms to diffuse and adapt them effectively—will determine whether and when countries can reap the benefits of AI.

By using 40 sub-indicators covering the three factors that influence the impact of AI—innovation, diffusion, and adaptation—a composite score can be calculated (see Fig. 1.4).

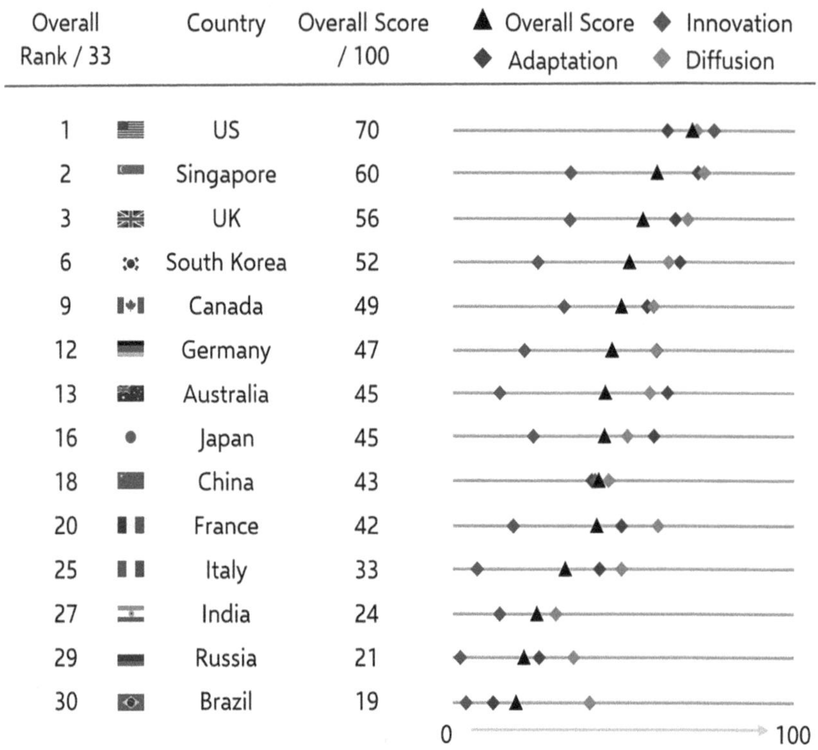

Fig. 1.4 AI Economic Impact Index (*Source:* Capital Economics, 2025)

Some existing definitions of AI, used by G20 economies in the introductory part of their AI modules, are provided below.

According to Eurostat, AI refers to systems using technologies such as: text mining, computer vision, speech recognition, natural language generation, machine learning, deep learning for gathering and/or using data to predict, recommend or decide the best action to achieve specific goals.

AI systems can be:

- purely software based, such as chatbots and business virtual assistants, which use: natural language processing; face recognition systems, with the help of computer vision or speech recognition systems; machine translation software; data analysis based on machine learning, etc.;

- embedded in devices, as autonomous robots for warehouse automation or production assembly works;
- autonomous drones for production surveillance or parcel handling, etc.

Statistics Canada (2019) says that AI refers to systems that display intelligent behavior by analyzing their environment and taking actions—with some degree of autonomy—to achieve specific goals. AI-based systems can be purely software-based or embedded in a device.

According to Aghion et al. (2019), AI includes all the technologies aiming at computerization of cognitive tasks traditionally performed by humans, voice recognition, biometrics, image recognition, decision support, etc.

AI is thus a branch of computer science studying the development of hardware and software systems having specific capabilities typical of the human being (interaction with the environment, learning and adaptation, reasoning, and planning), capable of pursuing autonomously a defined purpose, making decisions that until then were usually entrusted to people. In the words of Monostori (2014), 'AI is the science and engineering of making intelligent machines, especially intelligent computer programs.' AI systems show some traits of human intelligence such as learning, problem-solving, perception, and some creativity and social intelligence (Diaz-Rodríguez et al., 2023).

AI is a research field that studies the programming and design of systems aimed at providing machines with one or more characteristics that are considered typically human. Properties range from learning to visual or space-time perception. AI is a complex topic with many layers.

A 'true' AI machine can simulate human intelligence, behavior, and emotions. While no machine has still reached that level, modern AI can perform moderately complex functions. It can solve problems and decide using data inputs. In addition, it can recognize and interpret visual information as well as respond to written and verbal language. It can do so by using an enormous amount of information, thus being able to process new data, drawing unique, intelligent conclusions based on this information. The information it uses is entirely based on the sources supplied by humans. It is transformed into data and processed in ways that are often uncertain and can be often forecast with difficulty.

After the first studies of the 1950s, the expectations about AI began to increase, but, due to a lack of adequate computational devices, the concept of AI soon fragmented into distinct theories, which are still shared today and identify the first three types of AI:

1. Strong AI, according to which machines are capable of developing self-awareness, which studies systems capable of replicating human intelligence. This paradigm is supported by the research field of General AI (AGI), which studies systems capable of replicating human intelligence.
2. Artificial Narrow Intelligence (ANI), also known as Narrow AI or Weak AI, which believes it possible to develop machines capable of solving specific problems without being aware of the activities performed. The objective of this type is therefore not to create machines equipped with human intelligence, but to have systems capable of performing one or more complex human functions, such as voice assistants of the kind of Siri, Alexa, Google assistants, ChatGPT, which can perform a specific task, such as generating text responses to directions received.
3. Artificial Super Intelligence (ASI)—or Super AI—possibly to be considered as a way into the future, which will be achieved when AI is more capable than a human.

Let us gain a better understanding of each type.

1. AGI aims to build machines that think and would have the ultimate ambition to produce a machine whose overall intellectual ability is indistinguishable from that of a human being; it would represent generalized human cognitive abilities in software; therefore, even when faced with an unfamiliar task, the AGI system could find a solution.

AGI would be an intelligent system for computers and have comprehensive or complete knowledge and cognitive computing capabilities. This system would be indistinguishable from that of a human, except for the incredible high speed that today no existing computer can achieve. Such a system should be creative, have sensory perception, recognize colors, depth and three dimensions in static images, pinpoint a geographic location, etc. However, it can also cause dangers, as Stephen Hawking warned in 2014: ‘The development of full AI could spell the end of the human race. It would take off on its own and redesign itself at an ever-increasing rate. Humans, who are limited by slow biological evolution, couldn't compete and would be superseded.'

2. In contrast to AGI, ANI is in practical use today and is able to perform specific tasks or types of problems, by using a combination of machine learning, deep learning, reinforcement learning, and natural language processing (see below) for solving specific types of problems and executing specific focused tasks. It is goal-oriented without the ability of a self-expanding mechanism.

Examples of this type of AI include: customer service chatbots; voice assistants of the kind of Apple's Siri and Amazon's Alexa; recommendation engines (e.g., Google, Netflix, Spotify); self-driving cars, recognizing other vehicles, people and objects while adhering to driving rules and regulations; AlphaGo, a computer program that excels in a specific type of problem-solving.

There are different types of narrow AI: reactive AI, which is the basic version, with no memory or data storage capabilities, emulating the human mind's behavior and responding to different interpretations without any prior experience; limited Memory AI, more advanced, having great memory and data storage capabilities enabling machines to offer more precise interpretation using statistical data. Examples of narrow AI are: virtual assistants (e.g., Siri, Alexa, Cortana); IBM's Watson, which is capable of answering questions asked in natural language interpretations; Google's Rankbrain, an algorithm used to sort the search results; self-driven cars; facial/image recognition devices; drone-based robots.

Narrow AI has limitations due to its limited capabilities and the possibility of causing harm in case of a system failure, such as for self-driving cars, if they miscalculate the location or have a design flaw.

Another limitation might lie in the loss of jobs caused by narrow AI, but such a loss might be countered by an increase in the job opportunities in other fields.

3. Artificial superintelligence (ASI) would be capable of surpassing human intelligence by manifesting cognitive skills and developing emotional understanding, beliefs, skills, and desires of its own. It would be the most advanced, powerful, and intelligent type of AI, transcending every human being. Superintelligent machines would be self-aware and could have all the tasks humans can as well as non-human abstractions and interpretations.

Super AI Systems could imply threats, leading to a global catastrophe, due to loss of control and understanding. In fact, ASI systems could use their power and capabilities to carry out unforeseen actions and eventually become unstoppable, without the human possibility to contain them once they emerge or as they become the weapon of a government, a dictator, or social class or a corporation, and even sociopaths to unleash nuclear attacks, autonomous weapons, drones, and robots.

Super AI has, however, also potential advantages in reducing human error, being helpful in giving access to millions of programs. This can be done by: building logic from the available data on its own, compiling and debugging programs; replacing humans to accomplish risky tasks such as defusing a bomb, exploring the deepest parts of the oceans, coal, and oil mining, dealing with the consequences of natural or human-induced disasters; being always available; and for the possibility to explore new science frontiers (as for space travels).

At the time of the Chernobyl nuclear disaster, in 1986, superintelligent robots were not yet invented. If they were, they could intervene and eliminate the nuclear power plant's radiations, which were so intense as to kill any human approaching the place. Authorities were forced to pour sand and boron from a distance above by using helicopters. In addition, the healthcare industry could benefit significantly from super AI, which can play a pivotal role in drug discovery, vaccine development, and drug delivery, for example, for intracellular drug delivery.

Another advantage of super AI is that machines can be programmed to work 24 hours per 7 days a week, without any breaks, in contrast to human interventions. This could be done in a number of occupations from educational institutes to helpline centers.

Finally, space exploration could be facilitated by super AI, by testing and estimating the probability of success of many equations, theories, researches, rocket launches, and space missions.

In this scenario, AI must be treated by combining the theoretical aspects with the practical and operational ones.

Starting from the meaning of AI, we can here describe the main AI techniques (Machine Learning and Deep Learning above all). Examples of machine learning are speech and image recognition (e.g., when social media network can recognize faces), and protection from fraud. This is only possible because a system has been trained on large amounts of data, thus being able to learn from mistakes and devise predictions and decisions. After analyzing the various applications of AI, a question arises: how does AI work? There are different methodologies applied to this research field.

In fact, the applications and history of AI intersect with those of Machine Learning. If it is true that AI is configured as the study of the development of systems endowed with capabilities typical of human beings, Machine Learning can be considered a (very popular) path for the application of AI. We therefore refer to systems capable of learning from experience, with a mechanism similar to what a human being does from birth.

Based on the learning techniques, it is then possible to distinguish different types of Machine Learning, which can translate into different applications. The best known of these is certainly Deep Learning, but Machine Learning is much more multifaceted. In any case, by using Deep Learning technology, complex patterns can be recognized. Here, we look at its six main methodologies.

1. *Model prediction* or *predictive modeling* is an area of Machine Learning that includes a variety of techniques capable of gathering information from available data and learning models to apply to new data, which can be done by these models. Predictive Modelling therefore aims to make predictions about data or events in the future. This AI application channel is becoming increasingly popular in a number of companies and is especially applied in the field of fraud prevention, predictive maintenance, and qualitative analysis.
2. *Deep learning* is one of the most important areas of machine learning. It is a set of techniques that simulate the learning processes of the brain through layered artificial neural networks, in which each layer calculates the values for the next one. Simply put, Deep Learning is a learning technique in which artificial neural networks are exposed to vast amounts of data; these are then able to learn by themselves to perform certain tasks without the need for data preprocessing, such as speech and image recognition.
3. *Online learning*, also known as Real Time Machine Learning, is the branch of Machine Learning that studies techniques for problems in which data become available sequentially, one after another, and decisions must be made as a piece of data becomes available. Unlike Offline Learning, whose decisions are based on a previous acquisition of a set of data, learning and decision-making are interrelated

and interdependent: what is learned conditions the decisions, which condition the data that is observed for further learning.

4. *Explainable regression and classification* consists of Machine Learning techniques aimed at solving regression problems (prediction of ordinal quantities) and classification, such as to allow the explanation of the results obtained. In other words, explainable regression and classification allows one to understand why AI models for regression and classification make certain decisions following data processing, making this person to understand what happens in the 'black box' of Machine Learning.
5. *Information retrieval (IR)*. Information Retrieval is the set of techniques used to manage the representation, storage, organization, and access to objects containing information such as documents, web pages, online catalogs, and multimedia objects. The ultimate goal of these processes is to provide the user with information that he has previously searched for and which is, therefore, more relevant to his interests.
6. *Reinforcement learning*. Reinforcement learning is a machine learning technique aimed at solving sequential decision-making problems by achieving certain objectives through interaction with the environment in which it operates. An agent learning with reinforcement algorithms learns to make optimal decisions through an empirical trial-and-error approach. At each iteration the agent observes the environment through its sensors (physical or virtual), decides which action to perform, and observes the effects that the chosen action has had on the environment.

The impact of AI will certainly be very high. A specific subset of AI instruments, that is, those of generative AI,[5] will have a revolutionary impact on the various economies. McKinsey Global Institute estimates that it 'will add between $2.6 and $4.4 trillion in annual value to the global economy, increasing the economic impact of AI as a whole by 15 to 40%. ... Goldman Sachs predicts a 7%—or nearly $7 trillion—increase in global GDP attributable to generative AI.'

Figure 1.5 shows the possible applications of generative AI for an enterprise.

[5] Generative AI uses generative models to produce text, images, videos, or other forms of data. Major tools include generative AI chatbots such as ChatGPT, DeepSeek, Copilot, etc.

Artificial intelligence technologies play an important role in the digital era. 'This new revolution helps to improve, to reduce the cost and to speed up the production process, to transform the traditional models of interpersonal communication and interaction. For example, robotization leads to radical changes in the field of employment and foreign investment flows. Growing digital flows simplify the transfer of information and innovations all over the world. Therefore, everyone has a chance to participate in the global economic process. The more information is accumulated, the better and more productive decisions can be made on its basis. And the machine learning technologies using for information processing become more and more perfect' (Guryanova et al., 2021).

The use of AI technology in language learning, especially for cross-cultural communication, is essential and the AI technology offers benefits 'in language instruction, such as the provision of individualized feedback and interaction with both native and non-native speakers of the target languages.' 'Cross-cultural communication has gained significance in recent years as a result of the ubiquitous effects of globalization on interpersonal interactions. AI technology provides a solution to this issue by facilitating language exchanges and fostering intercultural dialogue' (Karakaş, 2023).

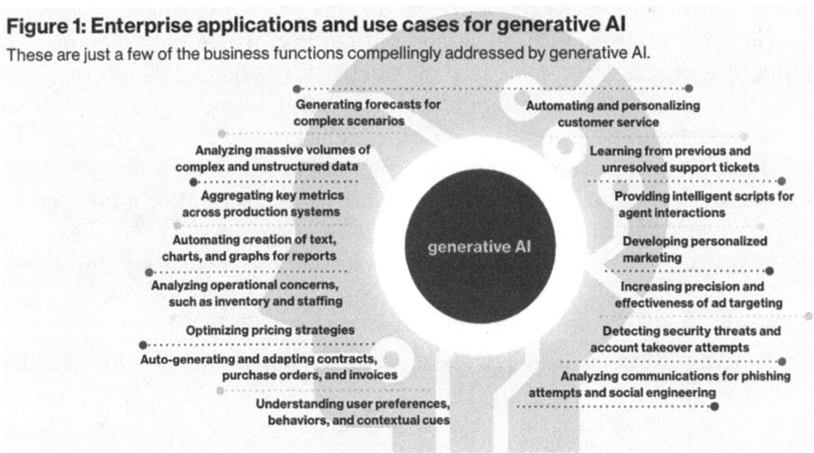

Fig. 1.5 Applications and uses of generative AI for firms (*Source:* MIT Technology Review Insights, 2023)

There are some ethical considerations surrounding AI deployment, due to: (1) biases in AI, deriving from the fact that AI learns from data, thus unintentionally perpetuating existing biases and unfair outcomes, such as biased hiring decisions or discriminatory lending practices; (2) frequent opaqueness of AI decision-making processes, reducing transparency and accountability and often leading to a 'black box'; businesses and policymakers must then establish clear guidelines to ensure AI systems are transparent, explainable, and accountable for their decisions; (3) possible concerns of data privacy and security, due to the fact that AI systems processing vast amounts of data and not always sensitive data are handled responsibly and in compliance with relevant regulations such as the General Data Protection Regulation (GDPR); (4) possible negative impacts on human dignity and autonomy, since 'relying too heavily on AI for decision-making in areas like healthcare and criminal justice could erode personal freedoms and fairness' (Thunderbird, 2024).

As for the country distribution of large-scale AI systems, Fig. 1.6 tells us that United States has the highest number, followed by China and, at a distance, other developed countries.

According to Bibi (2025), who follows Fortune Business Insights, the AI market is projected to grow from $515 billion in 2023 to $1.8 trillion by 2030. The growth will take place mainly in the United States, China, and the EU, which are investing 'heavily in AI research, infrastructure, and talent development to capitalize on this trend.' It will have applications in manufacturing, finance, and agriculture, which have significantly reduced their costs and increased productivity, thanks to AI.

Concerns for job displacements due to automation, are not justified as AI is also creating new opportunities, which should be, according to The World Economic Forum's 2023 report, of the order of 97 million in 2025. Obviously, job displacement creates problems that should be addressed by governments and organizations by reskilling programs.

AI is also redefining global trade dynamics and 'advanced algorithms enable real-time analysis of market trends, allowing businesses to make informed decisions.

On the diplomatic front, AI has become a critical tool for cybersecurity and strategic decision-making.' Nations are leveraging AI to monitor geopolitical developments, manage natural disasters, and enhance defense capabilities. However, this also raises ethical concerns about surveillance and data privacy, necessitating international cooperation to establish guidelines for responsible AI use.

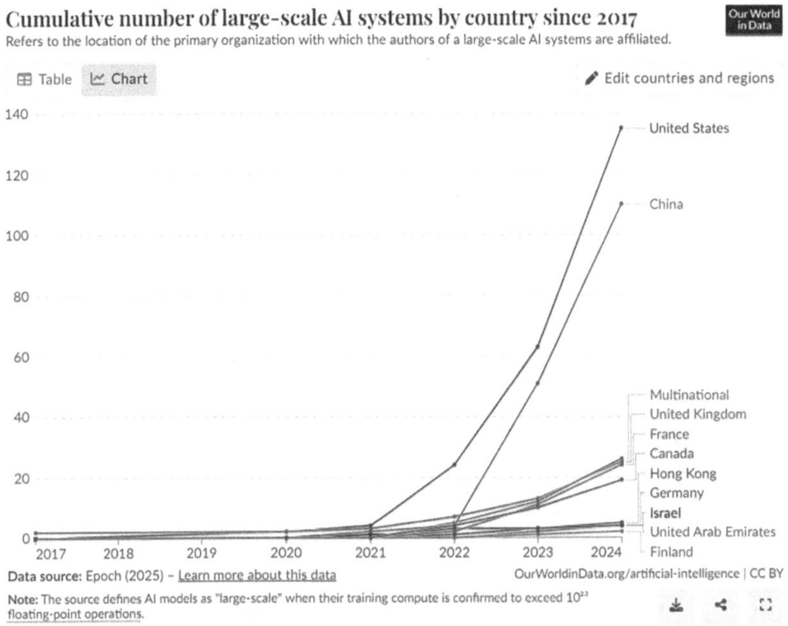

Fig. 1.6 Country-wise distribution of large-scale AI systems, 2017–2024 (*Source:* Giattino et al., 2023)

As AI adoption accelerates, it presents unique challenges. Issues such as algorithmic bias, data privacy, and the potential misuse of AI for malicious purposes require urgent attention. Governments and organizations worldwide are working on creating ethical frameworks and regulations to ensure AI is used responsibly.

References

Adel, A. (2022). Future of industry 5.0 in society: Human-centric solutions, challenges and prospective research areas. *J Cloud Comput (Heidelb), 11*(1):40. https://doi.org/10.1186/s13677-022-00314-5. Epub 2022 Sep 8. PMID: 36101900; PMCID: PMC9454409

Aghion, P., Antonin, C., & Bunel, S. (2019). Artificial intelligence, growth and employment: The role of policy. *Economie et Statistique / Economics and Statistics, 510-511-512*, 149–164. https://doi.org/10.24187/ecostat.2019.510t.1994

Alyoshina, I. V. (2019). *Artificial intelligence in an age of digital globalization.* chrome-extension://efaidnbmnnnibpcajpcglclefindmkaj/https://management-science.ru/site/public/elfinder/TEDS2019/TEDS2019-26-30-Alyoshina.pdf

Bibi, A. (2025, January 18). *The rise of artificial intelligence in shaping global economies.*https://moderndiplomacy.eu/2025/01/18/the-rise-of-artificial-intelligence-in-shaping-global-economies/

Bostrom, N. (2014). *Superintelligence: Paths, dangers, strategies.* Oxford University Press.

Capital Economics. (2025). *AI, economies and markets – How artificial intelligence will transform the global economy.* https://www.capitaleconomics.com/ai-economies-and-markets-how-artificial-intelligence-will-transform-global-economy#table-contents

Chandy, L., & Seidel, B. (2016, October 4). *Is globalization's second wave going to break? Brookings global economy and development.*

Daudin, J.-J., Li-Thiao Té, S., & Lebarbier, E. (2008). *Statistical challenges from the analysis of NGS-metagenomics experiments.* World Trade Organisation.

Díaz-Rodríguez, N., Del Serb, J., Coeckelbergh, M., López de Prado, M., Herrera-Viedma, E., & Herrera, F. (2023). Connecting the dots in trustworthy artificial intelligence: From AI principles, ethics, and key requirements to responsible AI systems and regulation. *Information Fusion, 99*, 1–24.

Giattino, C., Mathieu, E., Samborska, V., & Roser, M. (2023). *Artificial intelligence.* Published online at OurWorldinData.org. https://ourworldindata.org/artificial-intelligence

Global Transactions. (2020, January 16). *The impact of AI on global expansion.* https://www.globalization-partners.com/blog/the-impact-of-ai-on-global-expansion/

Guryanova, A. V., Shestakov, A. A., & Tikhonov, V. (2021). Digital globalization as a result of the modern economic and technological development. In S. I. Ashmarina, V. V. Mantulenko, M. I. Inozemtsev, & E. L. Sidorenko (Eds.), *Global challenges and prospects of the modern economic development* (European proceedings of social and behavioural sciences) (Vol. 106, pp. 787–792). European Publisher. https://doi.org/10.15405/epsbs.2021.04.02.94

Held, D., McGrew, A. G., Goldblatt, D., & Perraton, J. (1999). *Global transformations: Politics, economics, and culture.* Stanford University Press.

Ibrahim, I. A., Abdurrahman, I. A., & Baballe, M. A. (2025). Navigating the challenges of industry 5.0: How artificial intelligence is revolutionising the future of work. *Global Journal of Research in Engineering & Computer Sciences, 5*(3), 59–66. ISSN: 2583-2727. https://www.researchgate.net/publication/392129633

Jacks, D. S., & Tang, J. P. (2018). *Trade and immigration, 1870–2010.* NBER W. P, 25010. http://www.nber.org/papers/w25010

Karakaş, A. (2023). Chapter 12: Breaking down barriers with artificial intelligence (AI): Cross-cultural communication in foreign language education. In *Transforming the language teaching experience in the age of AI Publisher* (Vol. 99, pp. 214–234). IGI Global. https://doi.org/10.4018/978-1-6684-9893-4.ch012

Klasing, M. J., & Milionis, P. (2014). Quantifying the evolution of world trade, 1870–1949. *Journal of International Economics, 92*(1), 185–197. Available at SSRN: https://ssrn.com/abstract=2413883

Magistro, B., Borwein, S., Michael Alvarez, R., Bonikowski, B., & Loewen, P. J. (2025). Attitudes toward artificial intelligence (AI) and globalization: Common microfoundations and political implications. *American Journal of Political Science*, 1–18. https://doi.org/10.1111/ajps.12959

MIT Technology Review Insights. (2023). *The great acceleration: CIO perspectives on generative AI.* https://www.technologyreview.com/2023/07/18/1076423/the-great-acceleration-cio-perspectives-on-generative-ai/

Monostori, L. (2014). Artificial intelligence. In L. Laperrière & G. Reinhart (Eds.), *CIRP encyclopedia of production engineering*. Springer. https://doi.org/10.1007/978-3-642-20617-7_16703

Nordregio. (n.d.). *The three waves of globalisation.* https://archive.nordregio.se/en/Metameny/About-Nordregio/Journal-of-Nordregio/2008/Journal-of-Nordregio-no-1-2008/The-Three-Waves-of-Globalisation/index.html

Pedamkar, P. (2023). *Statistics for machine learning.* EDUCBA. https://www.educba.com/statistics-for-machine-learning/

Sociology Institute. (2023). *Sociology-of-development.* https://sociology.institute/sociology-of-development/

Statistics Canada. (2019). *Canada at a glance.* chrome-extension://efaidnbmnnnibpcajpcglclefindmkaj/ https://www150.statcan.gc.ca/n1/en/pub/12-581-x/12-581-x2019001-eng.pdf?st=b2VnDkJg

Thunderbird. (2024, October 25). *Global AI and the future of work.* https://thunderbird.asu.edu/thought-leadership/insights/global-ai-future-of-work

United Nations. (2024). *General Assembly adopts landmark resolution on artificial intelligence.* https://news.un.org/en/story/2024/03/1147831

West, D. M. (2018, October 4). *What is artificial intelligence?* https://www.brookings.edu/articles/what-is-artificial-intelligence/

Wodecki, A. (2019). *Artificial intelligence in value creation. Improving competitive advantage.* Palgrave Macmillan.

World Trade Organization. (2008). *World trade report 2008. Trade in a globalizing world.* https://www.wto-ilibrary.org/content/books/9789287044952/read

CHAPTER 2

The Effects of AI on Globalisation

Abstract We are now in the era of the fourth industrial revolution, which differs from all previous 'revolutionary' forms that took place during the world history, due to 'impressive innovations and powerful technological breakthroughs in various fields of science, technology, and production', such as 'the Internet of things', virtual environment, robotics, and other technological areas, for example, cognitive, cloud, bio-and nanotechnology. This fourth industrial revolution is fundamentally different from the previous ones: first of all, it has a higher speed of development and implementation of innovative technologies; secondly, it has a planetary, global scale of their distribution.

AI has both positive and negative effects. Among the former, the exponential growth of AI has emerged as a pivotal force reshaping the global landscape. AI-driven technologies are revolutionizing international trade. AI can also have a negative impact on some sections of a society. In fact, it can be expected to have critical social impacts, with significant variations across countries and regions.

Keywords Fourth industrial revolution • Internet of Things • Virtual environment • Robotics • Bio- and nanotechnology • Positive effects • Negative effects

N. Acocella, *The Economics of Globalization and Artificial Intelligence*, https://doi.org/10.1007/978-3-032-15711-9_2

Introduction

First of all, Guryanova et al. (2021) characterize the present era as 'the fourth industrial revolution,' following Schwab (2017). 'This revolution differs much from all previous "revolutionary" forms that took place during the world history,' due to 'impressive innovations and powerful technological breakthroughs in various fields of science, technology, and production,' such as 'the Internet of things, virtual environment, robotics, and other technological areas, such as cognitive, cloud, bio-and nanotechnology.' This fourth industrial revolution is fundamentally different from the previous ones: 'first of all, it has a higher speed of development and implementation of innovative technologies; secondly, it has a planetary, global scale of their distribution.'

Matyushok et al. (2021) identify and analyze the most important new trends in the world economy and investigate the effect of these key trends for the economy and society. In summary, 'technology and commerce have made data more valuable than material objects.'

As to the trends, the first one emerged from the end of twentieth century and 'is shown in relocating the center of business activities from the most developed countries to developing countries and markets, such as China, Brazil, and India, while keeping the leadership of the United States and other developed countries in the scientific-technical and world finance sphere.

The second trend is uncertainty growth in financial markets, capital outflow from developing markets to developed countries, and formation of new markets.

The third trend is neo-industrialization, which is an objective process of the newest industrial model formation based on high-technology structures. Neo-industrialization means primarily an economy based on knowledge, human resources, and networks. Computers, communications, and network technology dominate this new economy.

The fourth trend is the 'digitalization' of the world of people and the world of things, and the creation of a smart economy (new technology trends).

The fifth trend is the end of the era of hydrocarbon fuel, change in the structure of energy balances, and formation of new energy trends.

The sixth trend is the shift from a raw materials market to a services and technologies market.

One can think—following Rui and Bhaumik (2023)—of contemporary globalization as 'the product of new digital flows and an unstoppably developing phenomenon that will connect nations around similar interests, economics, and politics; and that, despite the problems, digitalization will still be able to encompass all regions of the world. In other words, globalisation is the result of new digital flows. In conclusion, the evidence suggests that contemporary globalisation is the result of new digital flows and a phenomenon that is unstoppably spreading and will unify states around comparable interests, economics, and politics.'

We can compare AI and human performance through time in a number of tasks, noting that in most of them AI has already reached and gone beyond the human one, such as for image classification, basic reading comprehension, visual reasoning (see Fig. 2.1).

We must then ask how wide is or will be the adoption of AI. According to the McKinsey Global Institute, by 2030 around 70% of companies will adopt at least one type of AI technology.

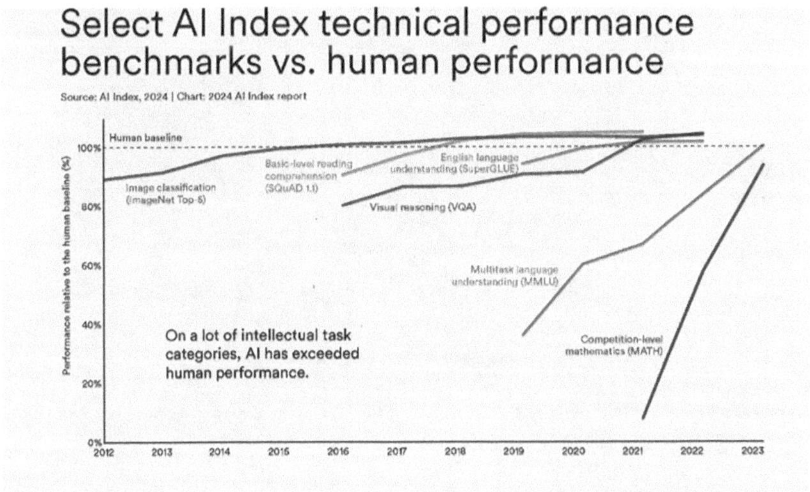

AI exceeds human performance on a selection of intellectual task categories. Image: Stanford University-AI Index

Fig. 2.1 AI technical performance versus human performance (*Source:* Fell, 2025)

As to the implications of this adoption, in 2018 Price Waterhouse Coopers predicted that by 2030 AI could increase global GDP by 14%, amounting to 1.2% additional GDP growth per year.

In a similar way, Fig. 2.2 shows the test scores of AI systems relative to human performance, in a number of capabilities.

AI impacts on globalization through:

1. increased productivity and economic growth and, thus, of international trade opportunities;
2. better management of complex and distant production units by providing a centralized management system;
3. expanded commerce via digital platforms.

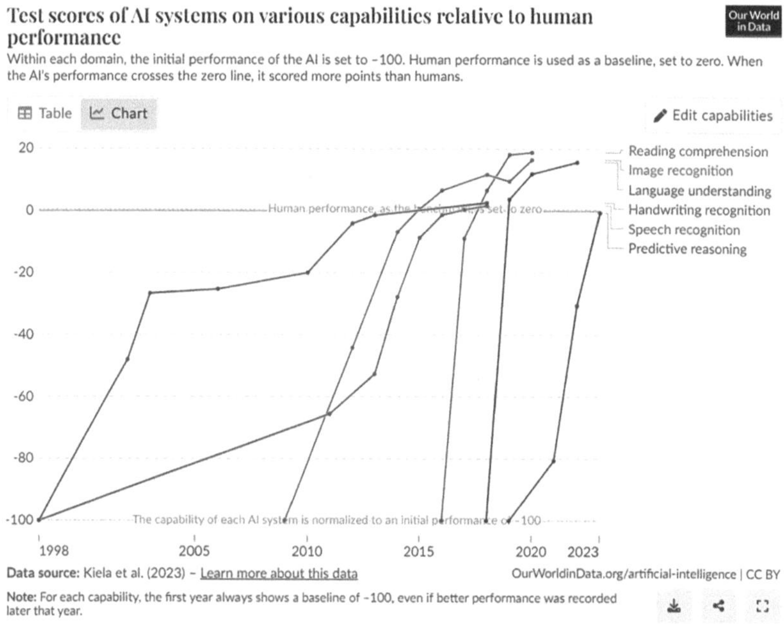

Fig. 2.2 Test scores of AI systems relative to human performance, in a number of capabilities (*Source:* Giattino et al., 2023). *Note:* The lines starting in 1998 indicate: Handwriting recognition (the one on the top) and Speech recognition; the one starting in 2009: Image recognition; the one starting in 2016: Reading comprehension; that starting in 2018: Language understanding and, finally, the one starting in 2019: Predictive reasoning

According to the McKinsey Global Institute by 2030, when at least 70% of companies will likely have adopted at least one form of AI technology, this has the potential to add 16%—or about $13 trillion—to the global economy and to increase GDP by 26% (McKinsey & Company Global Institute, 2023).

From another point of view, we must note the influence of AI on the globalized world. Steven Weber argues that we are heading toward a situation where 'global connectedness will not dissolve but will be defined by "regional" blocs, demarcated more by the rules and standards they follow than by territory. For leaders of firms and NGOs with global ambitions, navigating this transformation is the strategic challenge of the decade.' The world is not 'flattening out, offering a level playing field to organizations striving for worldwide reach. As global economic governance expanded, firms shifted operations to wherever was most efficient—designing in one country and buying, manufacturing, and selling in others. Today, the world looks bumpier, with rising protectionism, national struggles over data control, and tensions over who should set worldwide standards. Expect emerging regional blocs to be dominated by the major rule-makers: the US, China, and possibly the EU. Firms and NGOs will need to remake themselves by building complete, semi-independent organizations in each region. Every nation will choose which rule-maker it wants to align with, and it may not be the one next door. This new world has the potential to be more prosperous.' Weber argues, however, that friction between the dynamics of geography and technology will make it riskier (Weber, 2019).

The impact of AI has been profound on global issues such as, for example, agriculture, healthcare, and education. Its contribution to the global economy could be up to $15.7 trillion by 2030. However, the economic and social benefits of this technology tend to remain geographically concentrated, primarily in the Global North (North America) and China. Other countries will experience more moderate increases, due to a number of reasons: relative scarcity of technical infrastructures, models and tools, data, and talent and capacity; absence of policies and guidelines to ensure trustworthiness in regulating new technologies; much lower capacity to fund research and development to deploy the latest AI tools and lower rates of adoption of AI technologies. 'Indeed, an Oxford Insights assessment of 181 countries around the world and their preparedness in using AI in public services highlights that the lowest-scoring regions include much of the Global South, such sub-Saharan Africa, some Central and

South Asian countries, and some Latin American countries.' However, there is a commitment of countries in the Global South to use AI, as articulated in various national strategies such as AI For All from India.

Bendermacher and Moore (2024) note that 'for the globalization industry, the introduction of artificial intelligence (AI) at the beginning of 2023 was like an asteroid impact. This revolutionary technology has shaken the foundation of globalization and changed every aspect of our work lives. With large language models (LLMs) and neural machine translation (NMT) entering the market, AI has the potential to wipe out even the most consolidated and efficient globalization structures.'

By addressing the change with an open mind and insatiable thirst for understanding, this technology will present new opportunities for the evolution of globalization. Shaking us from our complacency, AI's arrival has forced us to consider new approaches. And some of them just might save us from total extinction.

A new, proprietary 'AI Economic Impact Index provides a tool for assessing which economies … are best placed to benefit from AI and its effects over the next couple of decades.'

As in Fig. 2.2 shown above, 'the US ranks first. This suggests that it will once again assume the role of the global technological leader as it has done for much of the past 100 or so years. This reflects its size, the rise in both private and public investment in R&D, and the rapid expansion of the higher education system.' Other countries follow at a distance. Notable is China's position, which only ranks eighteenth (see Capital Economics, 2025).

In other fields such as LMSYS Org, that is, Large Model Systems Organization, China has rapidly reduced its distance from the United States (see Fig. 2.3).

In order to understand the impact of AI on the labor market, Acemoglu and Restrepo (2018) provide a theoretical framework by decomposing the effect of new technologies on labor into three broad effects: a displacement effect, a productivity effect, and a reinstatement effect.

Frank et al. (2019) classify current literature on the labor market implications of AI into two broad categories: a doomsayer's perspective and an optimist's perspective. Doomsayers believe that labor substitution by AI will harm employment. Frey and Osborne (2013) estimate that 47% of total US employment is at risk of losing jobs to automation over the next decade. Their research reveals that a substantial share of employment in

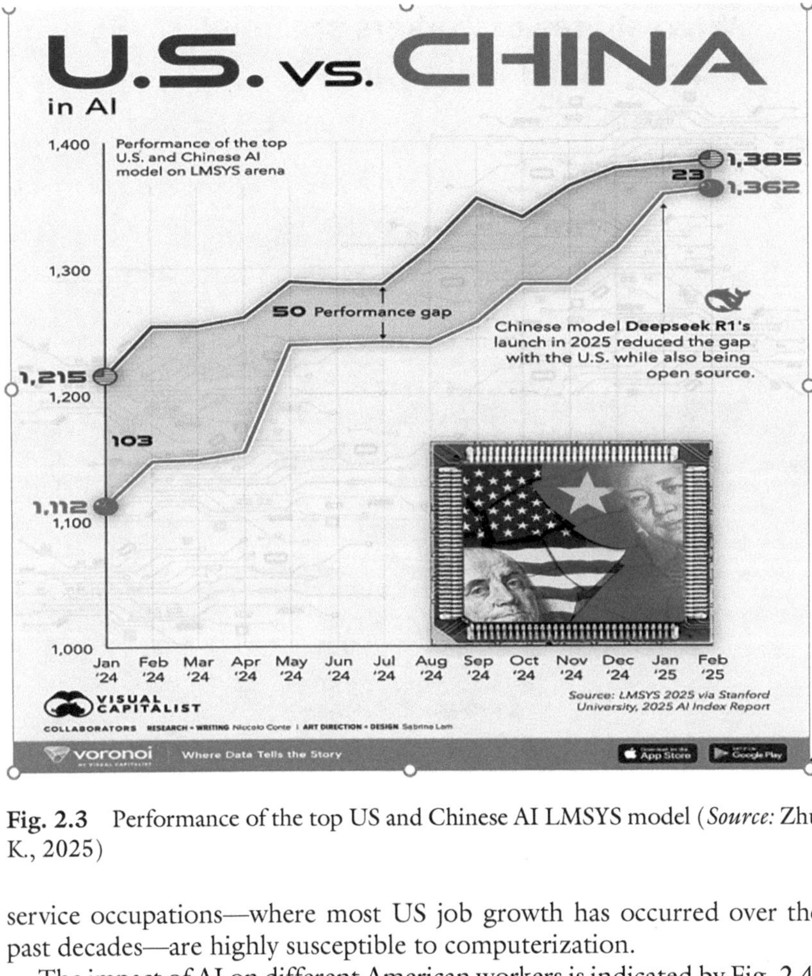

Fig. 2.3 Performance of the top US and Chinese AI LMSYS model (*Source:* Zhu K., 2025)

service occupations—where most US job growth has occurred over the past decades—are highly susceptible to computerization.

The impact of AI on different American workers is indicated by Fig. 2.4. This shows, at first sight astonishingly, that bachelors will be the workers most negatively affected. However, the surprise is not justified, if we consider what we have just said about the exposition of the share of employment in service occupations.

There will be stark differences across regions. While in high-income countries, 34% of jobs are exposed to GenAI, in low-income countries they are just 11%, with middle-income regions falling somewhere in

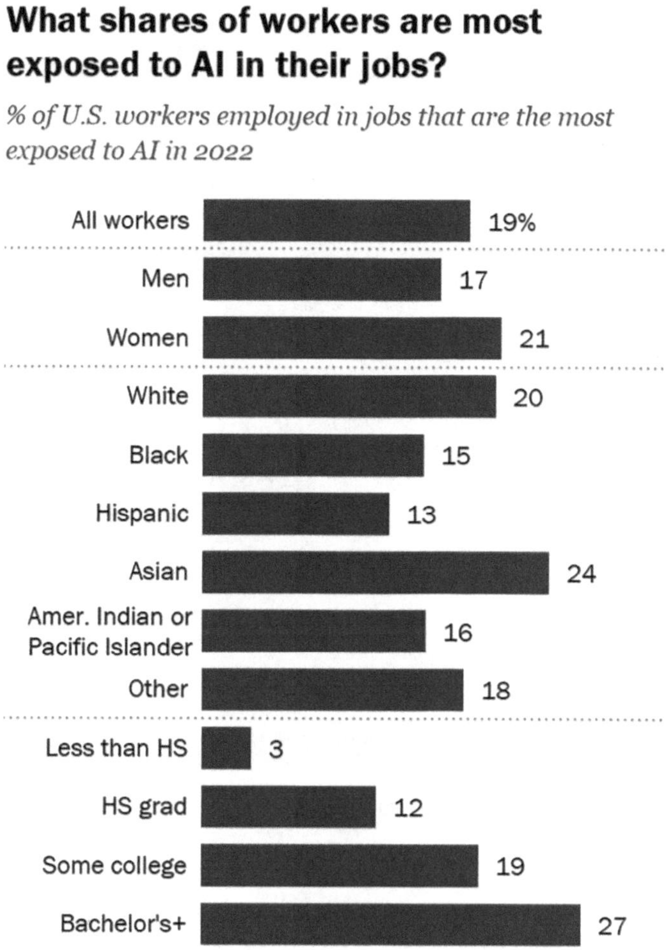

Fig. 2.4 Share of US workers most exposed to AI, 2022 (*Source:* Pew Research Center, 2023)

between. As to gender disparities, the most exposed one will be high female employment in clerical roles and widespread digital adoption, especially in Europe and Central Asia.

Regions such as sub-Saharan Africa, South Asia, and the Arab States currently show lower overall exposure but could still experience significant disruption in case of AI technologies spreading without safeguards.

A quarter of work tasks in the United States and Europe—or 300 million full-time jobs—could be replaced by AI. The workers exposed will be mainly educated white-collar workers earning up to $80,000 a year and two million manufacturing workers. Among the professions that will be mainly replaced by AI will be: customer service representatives, receptionists, accountants, sales people. By contrast, teachers, lawyers, judges, managers, and surgeons will not be affected (https://www.nexford.edu/insights/how-will-ai-affect-jobs).

While there is no clear relationship between AI exposure and employment growth, in occupations where computer use is high, greater exposure to AI is linked to higher employment growth. 'One possible explanation is that partial automation by AI increases productivity directly as well as by shifting the task composition of occupations towards higher value-added tasks. This increase in labour productivity and output counteracts the direct displacement effect of automation through AI for workers with good digital skills, who may find it easier to use AI effectively and shift to non-automatable, higher-value added tasks within their occupations.' Instead, workers with poor digital skills may not be able to interact efficiently with AI and thus reap all potential benefits of the technology (Georgieff & Hyee, 2022).

Guarascio and Reljic (2025) find that (a) AI is not universally beneficial or harmful, but has asymmetric effects across countries and occupations;[1] (b) positive employment outcomes are concentrated in countries having strong innovation systems.

Bowles (2014) uses Frey and Osborne's (2013) framework to estimate that 54% of EU jobs are at risk of computerization. Acemoglu and Restrepo (2018) provide a historical example of excessive automation negatively

[1] An example of the negative effects of AI is offered by West Africa, and particularly the Sahel, where misinformation and manipulation were spread by short videos generated by AI saying that some group was attacked by another group. The spread of fake news often derives from automated bots sharing content, political activists, or well-intentioned internet users who are duped.

affecting the labor market due to weak productivity and reinstatement effects, finding that areas in the United States most exposed to industrial automation in the 1990s and 2000s experienced large and robust negative effects on employment and wages.

AI is also expected to have a disruptive effect on the composition of the labor market. Autor (2015) presents evidence that the labor market has become polarized over the last few decades towards low-skilled and high-skilled jobs and away from medium-skilled jobs, due to the advent of computers. However, he states that this polarization is likely to be reversed, as some low- and medium-skilled jobs are likely to be relatively resistant to automation, while some highly skilled but relatively routine jobs may be automatable (potentially with technologies like AI). However, Brekelmans and Petropoulos (2020) conclude that, unlike the computer and robotic revolution, the AI revolution is unlikely to cause job polarization as it will affect low-skilled, middle-skilled, and high-skilled jobs.

Optimists believe that AI's productivity and reinstatement effects will be more than enough to compensate for the substitution effect. Some opinion pieces project that AI and robotics will have created up to 90 million jobs by 2025, indicating a strong positive labor market impact. The World Economic Forum concluded in October 2020 that while AI would likely take away 85 million jobs globally by 2025, it would also generate 97 million new jobs in fields ranging from big data and machine learning to information security and digital marketing.

As to the future development of the effects of AI, according to Provenzani (2024), the generative AI she consulted was able to identify ten predictions on what the world could be like in just over 25 years. These refer to: technological advances and AI (with AI and robotics even more integrated into daily life); climate change and sustainable energy (with widely used new technologies to mitigate the effects of climate change); new dynamics for work and education (with many professions that exist today that will be replaced by automation and AI); health and life expectancy (with significant improvements in health and life expectancy); globalization and connectivity (since these become more pervasive); urbanization and megacities (with several new megacities having advanced and sustainable infrastructures); shifts in global demographics (with many developed countries having an aging population, and developing countries having a younger population); food and sustainable agriculture (with innovations in agriculture critical to feeding a growing global population, vertical and urban farming, lab-grown meat and plant-based protein alternatives); revolution in transportation (with the advent of autonomous vehicles and advanced public transportation systems and electric and hydrogen vehicles); sharing economy and decentralization (with a sharing economy well established by 2050, and business models favoring the shared use of resources and services).

Schwalbe and Wahl (2020) note that developments of AI have raised hopes that it might help to address challenges unique to the field of global health in low- and middle-income countries have been frequently used for: diagnosis; patient morbidity or mortality risk assessment; disease outbreak prediction and surveillance; and health policy and planning. AI will then help to address challenges to global health and accelerate achievement of the health-related sustainable development goals. 'The global health community will need to work quickly to establish guidelines for development, testing, and use, and develop a user-driven research agenda to facilitate equitable and ethical use.'

Below we will first indicate the positive effects of AI on globalization, through reduction of costs, and also for (1) the reduced environmental consumption, (2) then its mixed effects and (3) its negative effects. Finally, we refer (4) to some policies needed for maximizing the positive effects of AI.

Positive Effects of AI on Globalization

Alabdulatif (2024) notes that the exponential growth of AI has emerged as a pivotal force reshaping the global landscape. AI has far-reaching implications across diverse realms, encompassing daily societal interactions, environmental sustainability, economic dynamics, and cybersecurity paradigms. AI can have a role in shaping smart cities, elucidating how intelligent systems optimize urban services, infrastructure, and overall quality of life. It can also play an instrumental role in fostering a sustainable environment, 'ranging from resource management to the mitigation of environmental threats,' employment structures, workforce dynamics, and broader economic landscapes, fortification of cybersecurity measures, highlighting its pivotal role in safeguarding digital ecosystems against evolving threats.[2]

[2] An ecosystem is a system of organisms and their environment, linked by nutrient cycles and energy flows. On the positive effect of AI for the analysis of the environment, see Francisco (2023).

In fact, AI-driven technologies are revolutionizing international trade by: streamlining logistics and supply chains; optimizing shipping routes, inventory management, and customs processes; reducing costs and delays; facilitating online marketplaces through AI-powered platforms connecting buyers and sellers across borders and thus removing geographical barriers and expanding market reach; enhancing trade negotiations through AI aids in data analysis and modelling and providing insights that inform negotiation strategies and improve outcomes.

AI and related technologies such as the Internet of Things (IoT) can foster progress in ecological and biodiversity research, even if field ecologists could find reduced demand for their services. Drones equipped with AI technologies can be used to combat deforestation or poaching, as happened In Kenya, where drones track poachers in the Maasai Mara. However, poachers could use the same technologies for their own advantage. Drones equipped with AI technologies can also combat deforestation or can be used in agriculture, for helping farmers monitor their crops and livestock.

In France public authorities are increasingly using AI for the digital transformation of public services.

AI and new digital technologies are also transforming digital trade, as 'they facilitate the development of new business models of trade and reduce the geographical barriers of economic transactions.' These transformations are particularly useful for the small and medium enterprises. Their adoption varies a great deal across countries, including within the EU. 'Digital trade is not new, but it is taking new forms that are ushering a new phase of globalisation. So far digital trade mainly affected trade in goods, including through global value chains (GVCs), though some service activities have already become more tradeable thanks to digital technologies. The new phase of globalisation driven by AI and new digital technologies is likely to do for services what the previous phase did for manufacturing: to vastly increase trade between advanced and emerging economies.' A number of important issues for domestic policies and trade policy arise from that—in particular, by using tools like Google's Neural Machine Translation and Microsoft Translator—such as the possibility to connect individuals living or operating in different places. These include cross-cultural education platforms; real-time translation tools connecting remote teams; cross-cultural education platforms using AI to teach language and customs.

Together with positive effects on jobs, AI has similar effects on the level of GDP. The most profound impact of generative AI may be on economic growth. The effects on world regions are presented in Table 2.1.

Goldman Sachs's research estimates a baseline case in which the widespread adoption of AI could contribute 1.5% to annual productivity growth over a ten-year period, lifting global GDP by nearly $7 trillion. The upside case carries a remarkable 2.9% total uplift. But these outcomes are not guaranteed and will be determined by four key components: energy, compute, data and models (Greenbaum et al., 2023).

Indeed, as Ilzetzki and Suryaansh (2023) note, use of AI for day-to-day tasks has increased and AI has revealed to be an engine of productivity and growth. It will increase global economic growth by 4–6% per annum in the upcoming decade, even if not affecting employment rates in high-income countries. A similar effect is noted by Dias da Silva and Weißler (2025).

Ratten (2024) examines how AI has facilitated internationalization by reducing costs and raising time efficiency, improving stakeholder engagement, and becoming part of global business practices.

Meltzer (2018) writes that 'as to the impact on the structure of economic systems, AI is likely to accelerate the transition towards services economies', by making business 'use AI to improve warehouse management, demand prediction, and improve the accuracy of just-in-time manufacturing and delivery .... Business can also use AI to improve physical inspection and maintenance of assets along supply chains. The development of GVCs will be affected by the broader trends toward using AI in

Table 2.1 Impact of AI on GDP worldwide in 2030, by region

Region	*GDP growth due to AI in %*	*GDP growth due to artificial intelligence in trillions of US dollars*
China	26.1	7
North America	14.5	3.7
Southern Europe	11.5	0.7
Developed Asia	10.4	0.9
Northern Europe	9.9	1.8
Latin America	5.4	0.5
The rest of the world	5.6	1.2

Source: Duhienko and Sulieimanova (2024)

order to develop smart manufacturing. For instance, the German-led conception of industry 4.0 is based on sensors, IoT, and cyber-physical-systems that connect machines, material, supplies, and customers.'

García (2024) underlines the many advantages derived from AI in a globalized world. AI will reshape the global labor landscape, from eliminating language barriers to enhancing remote work and automating physical tasks. Automatic translation tools, project management platforms, and automation solutions will enable companies to operate more flexibly and efficiently without worrying about geographical boundaries. AI will also facilitate the massive personalization of training and professional reskilling, helping workers adapt to technological and economic changes while allowing companies to access a more diversified global talent pool. However, this technological revolution also presents significant challenges, such as the reduction of low-skilled jobs and changes in migration patterns. Therefore, AI offers enormous opportunities, but its implementation must be managed prudently to maximize its benefits and minimize its drawbacks. The globalization of labor markets, driven by AI, has the potential to create a more interconnected, efficient, and fair world, but it requires all involved parties to pay constant attention to the ethical, cultural, and social aspects of this transformation.

Fornes and Altamira (2023) notice that AI has shown 'a positive contribution to business performance while supporting international expansion of firms.' They add that the positive impact of AI 'is developing gradually and will only be evident in the medium term.' They also analyze today's major challenges in: '(i) widening the gap in the adoption and implementation of AI among countries, companies, and workers, and (ii) adapting trade rules and regulations to a context increasingly influenced by new technologies.'

Wang et al. (2023) show that 'AI has a significant inhibitory effect on ecological footprints.' From their analysis, referred to the period 2010–2019, it derives that 'AI significantly reduced the global ecological footprint, which highlights its key role in promoting sustainable development' (and) 'after constructing instrumental variables to address potential endogeneity issues and performing a series of robustness tests, this conclusion remains robust.' This conclusion holds even after endogeneity and robustness tests.

Therefore, the government should continue to support the research on AI and its applications, 'promote the cross-industry integration of AI, and play a positive role in the process of globalization to promote global sustainable development.'

According to Baviera (2025), AI 'is now one of the key technologies in global competition, on a par with the control of trade routes or the securing of supply chains for production. The risk is that it "could generate new asymmetries of power," on a par with the control of trade routes or the securing of supply chains for production.' Today, AI can generate new asymmetries of power. 'It is in fact a dual-use technology, with both civil and military effects, capable of establishing the scientific and, consequently, political-economic primacy of a power. This explains why the main international players are trying not to miss the innovation train.'

AI associated to globalization has a high impact on the course of the economy. In fact, Saeed and Sofi (2025) find that the Globalization Index, the AI Adoption Rate, and FinTech Integration significantly influence both financial performance and customer satisfaction. Specifically, FinTech Integration showed the strongest positive impact, followed by the AI Adoption Rate and the Globalization Index. This study demonstrates that enhancing globalization efforts, adopting AI technologies, and integrating FinTech solutions are crucial strategies for improving financial performance and customer satisfaction in Pakistan's banking sector post-COVID. This high impact of globalization, AI, and FinTech Integration is confirmed by Iqbal and Fikri (2025).

Barrot (2024) rightly notes that 'the current challenges in global higher education, ranging from uneven quality distribution to limited access, funding constraints, and inadequate integration of technology, underscore the urgent need for innovative solutions.' The need arises of enhancing teaching and learning, including personalized assistance, language learning support, efficient writing assistance, and automated feedback. At the same time, limitations arise: potential negative impacts on academic integrity; inaccuracy; lack of emotional depth; risk of social isolation. These risks must be addressed for responsible integration. He suggests a set of principles for integration such as: academic integrity, fair assessment, continuous monitoring, support mechanisms, and the promotion of human creativity.

We must add that the rise of AI leverages complex information and provides more refined projections than those of classical models, by integrating large amounts of real-time data (on mobility, environment, and social networks). We must say, however, that AI projections have some limitations, such as a lack of transparency, high data requirements, and the risk of unequal access to the technology. Thus, traditional models must be used together with those powered by AI (Perlant, 2025).

According to Team GP (2020), in the future, there are many ways in which AI is likely to impact global expansion, that is, by improving predictions of future trends, increased automation of tasks, more reliable autonomous vehicles, greater accuracy and efficiency, greater focus on business innovation, cost-effectiveness. Since a global company's success largely relies on its ability to predict and respond to future trends, accurate predictions of these trends with predictive modeling done by AI can be of help, 'enabling companies to make more informed decisions as they expand into international markets.'

AI systems put greater focus on business innovation than on routine, everyday processes, which frees up the mental and creative resources of managers, making them to do higher-level work.

It increases automation of tasks. 'In human resources processes, for example, automation can help streamline recruiting, onboarding, training, payroll, and benefits provision. And more sophisticated forms of AI will likely be able to analyze tax laws and international regulations much more quickly and efficiently than humans can. Automating these processes with AI will help companies save time and labor and reduce their vulnerability to sanctions.'

From the point of view of manufacturing, AI can enable constant production, day and night, which increases productivity. AI's sensory systems, along with its decreased dependence on human operators, can also increase safety on the shop floor. As AI becomes more sophisticated, it can greatly improve smart manufacturing, which requires interconnectivity between sensor systems, computer systems, and physical machinery, by specializing and streamlining specific processes.

AI can ensure more reliable autonomous vehicles, or self-driving cars, which have many sensors, especially radar and light detectors, that collect information about objects around the vehicle and make the AI system use this data to make instant decisions about the best way to drive. These cars are less expensive, for a number of reasons.

AI is more cost-effective than human employees because it requires only a purchase cost, does not require a salary, raises, health benefits, or pension contributions.

In the field of healthcare, AI has revolutionized medical diagnosis, thanks to advanced imaging systems analyzing radiological images and scans to detect pathologies with a precision that was unthinkable until a few years ago. In addition, pharmaceutical research is using AI to accelerate the development of new drugs as it allows to identify potential compounds more quickly and model molecular interactions with unprecedented precision.

In the context of the financial economy, AI has become a powerful weapon for data analysis and market forecasting. AI-based predictive models are used to identify financial trends, manage risk, and optimize the investment portfolio, all of which give financial operators a deeper and instantaneous understanding of global markets.

Last but not the least, AI is revolutionizing the education sector, through the personalization of learning through intelligent tutoring systems, but also with the adaptation of the study path to the individual needs of students and easier access to education through increasingly advanced digital platforms and tools. (Vezzoli, 2024).

Even if AI's impact on global growth will be positive, due to the productivity gains, which could lift global GDP by up to 4% in a high Total Factor Productivity (TFP) growth scenario over the next decade, the gains will not be evenly distributed, with advanced economies benefitting disproportionately, which reflects their stronger AI preparedness and exposure, greater access to high-tech infrastructure and data. Indeed, the estimated growth impact in advanced economies (and, notably, the United States) could be more than double than in low-income countries. These results depend on a number of factors such as policy action, stronger institutions, and digital infrastructures (Cerutti et al., 2025).

Mixed Effects of AI on Globalization

The effects of AI in a globalized world will be different for the different sexes in the various countries: in high-income countries, where clerical jobs[3]—which are most exposed to generative AI technology—make up a greater proportion of occupations—'the effects are more striking: 2.9% of men's jobs compared with 7.8% of women's jobs,' as women are more represented in clerical jobs, with respect to a total 1.4% of men's jobs,

[3] While the potential for job displacement from AI is not huge, it is concentrated. Clerical support workers, with 58% of tasks in this occupation, have medium-level exposure and 24% have high-level exposure. This stands in contrast to other occupational groups, in which the largest share of highly exposed tasks oscillates between 1% and 4%, and medium-exposed tasks do not exceed 25%.

compared with 3.7% of women's employment globally (United Nations Regional Information Centre for Western Europe, 2025).

There are cases of AI bringing both positive and negative effects in a globalized world. In fact, together with a superabundant world, with unprecedented human freedom created by AI, there are fears of malicious superintelligence and killer robots, carrying political and economic risks. AI can thus break democratic and egalitarian institutions, similarly to what did the colonialism, in terms of cultural devastation of indigenous societies. However, measures can be suggested to ensure that AI has widespread benefits. 'Competition policy emerges as a critical tool, as do adaptive changes to political institutions. Without appropriate measures, there may be no AI-driven growth takeoff and the inequality that emerges would dwarf anything experienced to date' (Carvalho, 2025).

Cazzaniga et al. (2024) find that almost 40% of global employment is exposed to AI, which affects income and wealth inequality. AI displacement risks extend to higher-wage earners, whereas in previous waves of automation the strongest effects were on middle-skilled workers. The effects on labor income inequality largely depend on whether and to the extent to which AI displaces or complements high-income workers.

Stiglitz and Korinek (2025) recognize that AI can offer benefits in terms of technological advances, but argue that our global system of economic governance must be reformed. In fact, 'progress in artificial intelligence and related forms of automation technologies threaten to reverse the gains that developing countries and emerging markets have experienced from integrating into the world economy over the past half century, aggravating poverty and inequality.... (in fact) ... the new technologies have the tendency to be labor-saving, resource-saving, and to give rise to winner-takes-all dynamics that advantage developed countries.' There are, however, economic policies that would mitigate the adverse effects on developing and emerging economies while leveraging the potential gains from AI.

As to the effects of AI on globalization, we can say that it has contributed to increased inequality inside many countries, while reducing it between countries, partly due to Chinese growth and some of its positive effects in other developing nations. By contrast, the machine learning economy tends to shape a different inequality landscape, by creating first-mover advantages, positive feedback growth loops, etc., which create superstar economies. 'This looks like very bad news for poor developing countries, who can no longer count on low-cost manufacturing as the first rung of a ladder to faster growth.'

Some AI technologies—from facial recognition to automated online surveillance—can enhance the power of states and corporations to suppress activism.

The globalization of AI can advance environmental knowledge and conservation. 'The consequences of AI for environmentalism are highly variable, empowering some campaigns and depowering others … Going forward, AI technologies would seem set to advance technocratic, incremental, and moderate forms of environmentalism while hampering confrontational tactics and grassroots resistance, especially in authoritarian states. At the same time, AI is going to spur wasteful consumption, natural resource extraction, and the production of electronic waste. The globalization of AI, as these findings reveal, is set to unsettle the politics of environmentalism, doing some good, but bringing many dangers' (Dauvergne, 2021).

AI could widen the gap between LDCs and the developed world. However, also the former can draw some positive results from it. In particular, this is the case of healthcare systems, where this technology can integrate doctors' work, 'giving them the opportunity to treat more patients more efficiently … by helping them to identify a disease and to provide the best possible treatment for it. This would be particularly important for the developing world where there is a shortage of specialized education and medical expertise.' AI is also used to compare medical product prices, as happens in India.

> AI can also prove vital in assisting educational systems in emerging countries by helping teachers to better plan the study process and select appropriate learning approaches. There is also potential for study methods to be adapted and tailored to students' needs. (Development Aid, 2023)

In addition, as the World Bank (2020) says, AI could be helpful in the field of infrastructures and energy. By combining 3D printing with AI technologies low-budget houses can be built. There are also real-world scenarios for AI use in the energy sector, for example, for optimizing electricity consumption.

In addition, more accurate weather forecasts promoted by AI can bring positive effects for agriculture, especially in developing countries. AI could also be used to identify the plants 'best suited for certain areas, to select the right pesticides, or to design irrigation systems.'

There are also potential negative impacts of AI on the LDCs, as in the case these apply the same technologies—such as robotics—that are used in developed countries, where, however, there are different wage conditions. Here we must note that the deepening of capital and the refinement of the division of labor that has been introduced into industrial enterprises through the use of robotics have successfully mitigated the damaging impact of the adoption of robot technology on employment. 'Rather than the traditional perceptions of robotics crowding out labour jobs, the overall impact on the labour market has exerted a promotional effect' (Shen & Zhang, 2024).

According to Development Aid (2023) AI is expected to have the highest effect in the job market of the LDCs, due to the use of the market of these countries by advanced economies for outsourcing, mainly in manufacturing and logistics. 'AI may also impact services that involve more creativity which are not automatic, for instance, the customer support sector which has long utilized outsourcing.'

However, a negative impact is derived due to the lack of access to AI solutions in LDCs. 'For example, according to International Telecommunication Union, in Africa, only 40% of the population uses the internet. ... Since AI is data-driven and needs a constant online connection, in the long run, the lack of access to the internet could result in certain parts of the world being isolated from the technological advances that AI is expected to bring.'

Another effect of AI in a globalized world is 'the pivotal shift from mainstream media as the traditional agenda-setting powerhouse to technology giants, including Google, Microsoft, Meta (formerly Facebook), and TikTok. This shift is significant as it marks a departure from established media conglomerates' paradigms of agenda setting. Technology companies utilize advanced algorithms and LLMs to identify, shape, and amplify trends, effectively influencing the shared global culture.'

This transformation has far-reaching consequences. A risk arises that 'dominant narratives will be perpetuated, non-Western perspectives will be marginalised, and cultural diversity will be eroded. Echo chambers are becoming more intense, contributing to societal polarisation and division. The decline of traditional media dominance and the loss of human editorial judgement exacerbate these issues' (Sichach, 2023).

Miguelañez (2025) notes that 'LLMs can learn new tasks on the fly, without requiring any explicit training or parameter updates. This mode of using LLMs is called in-context learning. It relies on providing the model with a suitable input prompt that contains instructions and/or examples of the desired task. The input prompt serves as a form of conditioning that guides the model's output.

The process of designing and tuning the natural language prompts for specific tasks, with the goal of improving the performance of LLMs is called prompt engineering. Effective prompt engineering can significantly improve the performance of LLMs on specific tasks. It's done by providing instructions and contextual information that help guide the model's output. Researchers can steer the LLM's attention toward the most relevant information for a given task by carefully designing prompts, leading to more accurate and reliable outputs.'

There are however potential risks, particularly for fundamental freedoms, which justifies the adoption of rules at both the national and European levels. Such risks are, firstly, that the use of AI could undermine certain fundamental freedoms, due to the fact that the effectiveness of AI often depends on the massive exploitation of personal data. In addition, when AI is deployed in public spaces, its use presents risks not only to privacy, but also to other freedoms. The case of augmented video surveillance (AVS) is interesting in this respect because the use of AI, trained on millions of hours of streaming images of people and capable of analyzing in real time the images filmed by the approximately 90,000 cameras installed across our country, allows for the development of widespread surveillance of individuals.

AI can also exhibit significant discriminatory biases because algorithms reproduce the subjectivity of the data they are fed, or even increase it due to their scale of deployment. The Compas algorithm used in the American judicial system to decide whether or not to release prisoners based on the risk of recidivism, for example, is fed with seemingly neutral and perfectly legal data. In reality, they convey racial discrimination resulting from the exploitation of old decisions, marked by racial prejudice: because the algorithm reproduces pre-existing biases, African-American prisoners have higher scores for risk of recidivism than Caucasian prisoners (see Engel et al., 2025).

Cluzel-Metayer (2024) notes that among the risks deriving from AI there is, first of all, the one deriving from the fact that the use of AI could undermine certain fundamental freedoms; in addition, there are possible privacy violations (e.g., when AI is deployed in public spaces, its use poses risks to privacy and also to other freedoms). 'The case of augmented video surveillance (AVS) is interesting in this respect because the use of AI, trained on millions of hours of streaming images of people and capable of analyzing in real time the images filmed by the approximately 90,000 cameras installed across our territory, enables the development of widespread surveillance of individuals.' AI impacts not only the right to privacy, but also freedom of movement, freedom of expression, demonstration, and conscience. Feeling watched leads to the so-called 'chilling effect.' In addition, use of AI exhibits significant discriminatory biases because algorithms reproduce the subjectivity of the data they are fed, or even exacerbate them due to their scale of deployment. 'The Compas algorithm used in the American judicial system to decide whether or not to release prisoners based on the risk of reoffending.' In addition, the energy cost of AI, which has risen sharply with the widespread use of its applications, cannot be underestimated in the context of global warming.

Finally, there are positive and negative impacts of AI technologies on some crucial cognitive functions, such as: attention, memory, addiction, novelty-seeking and perception, decision-making, and critical thinking, as well as learning abilities. These effects are different for different age groups and there are some unique challenges and benefits for all ages (Shanmugasundaram & Tamilarasu, 2023).

Negative Effects of AI on Globalization

AI can have a negative impact on some sections of a society. In fact, it can be expected to have critical social impacts, having significant variation across countries and regions. AI systems have 'demonstrated a pattern of exacerbating inequality, often in the most unequal societies and particularly for the most vulnerable populations. While AI-based technologies offer enormous promise to better the lives of people everywhere, they also bring risks. The unwanted social impacts of AI may be felt most immediately by historically marginalized groups, but they are unlikely to be limited to any particular group' (Hagerty & Rubinov, 2019).

According to Rana (2022), AI may have a considerable impact on the job market, resulting 'in increased inequality, lower salaries, and a smaller tax base. Although these concerns are still valid, there is debate about whether and how much the dangers will materialise. They are not a given, and careful policy might encourage the development of AI while limiting the negative effects. The EU has the chance to improve its standing in the international market and direct AI in a way that benefits its people and economy. In order to accomplish this, it must first agree on a joint strategy that would work to its benefits and permit member states to aggregate their assets across several industries. Therefore, artificial intelligence is having a variety of effects on the economy.'

Georgieva (2024) notes that in emerging markets and low-income countries AI exposure is expected to be lower, 40% and 26%, respectively, thus facing fewer immediate disruptions from AI. However, these 'countries don't have the infrastructure or skilled workforces to harness the benefits of AI, raising the risk that over time the technology could worsen inequality among nations.'

Technological advancements have been harnessed for warfare. In fact, AI is often used to power autonomous weapons, such as drones or robots. This means that countries can easily get involved in conflicts in which they may use AI-powered autonomous technology 'for reducing or deflecting human responsibility in decision-making and, in addition, for aiming to reduce human soldiers deaths, which by itself is a humane thing to do, but makes it politically easier to start wars' (Caruso, 2024).

Kanungo (2023) deals with the rising concern about the negative impact on the environment of the AI and notes that society can effectively address concerns about it, in order to strive for a sustainable future. She delves 'into the environmental impact of AI, exploring associated problems including carbon emissions, electronic waste, and potential harm to ecosystems' and examines 'how society can effectively address these concerns and strive for a sustainable future where AI and environmental preservation go hand in hand.'

Cornelli et al. (2023) devise a global panel, which shows that investment in AI is associated with: higher-income inequality, greater productivity, and a shift to high-tech services, which can often be traded across borders. In particular, higher-income households have seen their incomes and income shares increase, while there has been a decline in the income shares of households in the fifth and bottom deciles. In addition, there is 'a positive association of modern services exports and total factor productivity to AI. In labour markets, there is a contraction in overall employment, a shift from mid-skill to high-skill managerial roles and a reduced labour share of income.'

In addition to what Cornelli et al say, we must consider that implementation, incorporation, and effective use of the new technologies of the AI takes time, which implies that productivity growth will increase further, due to the AI technologies already implemented.

Francescato (2018) says that it is dangerous to adopt international metrics of productivity as the main indicator of success. In fact, for example, if a school program is evaluated by the test results achieved by students, teachers will tend to concentrate on teaching students how to perform a good test result, thus corrupting the educational process.

The use of AI raises fundamental ethical questions, as underlined by the Amnesty International (2019) report, since business models based on the mass collection of data threaten privacy and human rights. In addition, 'algorithms can perpetuate bias and discrimination if they are not carefully developed. Cases of facial recognition systems that incorrectly identify people of color or recruitment algorithms that discriminate against women are just the tip of the iceberg. The European Union, through the GDPR and the Artificial Intelligence Act, is trying to set global standards for ethical and responsible AI. But in a globalized world, can the laws of a single bloc really make a difference if others do not follow?'[4]

The implications of having a small handful of countries controlling cutting-edge AI in the future are profound. Among the negative effects of AI we can include the implications of having a few countries controlling cutting-edge AI in the future. As Wagner (2018) says, 'on one hand, these technologically advanced countries could become the de facto guardians of AI, ensuring that significant resources are devoted to its development on a long-term basis. It is also certain that leading companies in these countries will achieve and maintain an even more noteworthy lead in the global economic arena, granting them a substantial competitive advantage. The militaries of these countries would also almost certainly become primary beneficiaries of the AI technologies of the future, spurring a global race for superior autonomous weaponry and propelling the world toward dangerous new means of waging war.'

Following this suggestion, one can refer to what Lanzi (2025) says about the risks of a 'Malthusian dynamics' for poor countries due to the AI revolution, because AI-based automation will increase inequality and poverty levels within and between developing countries, arresting or reversing their economic convergence with developed countries.

[4] GDPR is General Data Protection Regulation, a rule applicable as of May 25, 2018, in all EU member states to harmonize data privacy laws across Europe.

Gale and Null (2025) correctly note that, 'while AI offers many promises, particularly in medicine and improving the lives of the disabled, it also threatens to displace millions of American workers across nearly every sector of the economy. This is not a distant scenario. According to a comprehensive report by the McKinsey Global Institute, nearly 39 to 73 million American jobs could be lost to AI automation by 2030 ... While some workers will be retrained or moved into newly created roles, a significant portion will face permanent banishment ... These job losses won't be distributed evenly. Workers in low- and middle-wage positions are most likely to feel the effects. Moreover, educational disparities will deepen as younger, less-educated, and rural populations become disproportionately affected ... The cost will not only be borne by job losses but in rising inequality and civil unrest. Economic mobility will be stripped away for tens of millions of Americans and their families.'

There is also a problem of political dominance in the development and implementation of AI. Currently this role pertains to the United States, which can raise concerns for the rest of the planet. According to Quiroga Rodríguez, 'a US-centric AI may reflect and reinforce American values, interests, and policies, which are often at odds with the needs and priorities of other regions, due to the simple learning bias of that AI.'

Eliezder Yudkowsky, who is a leading US decision theorist, wrote in 2023: 'The key issue is not "human-competitive" intelligence (as the open letter puts it); it's what happens after AI gets to smarter-than-human intelligence. Key thresholds there may not be obvious, we definitely can't calculate in advance what happens when, and it currently seems imaginable that a research lab would cross critical lines without noticing' (Yudkowsky, 2023).

Czarnecki T. (2024) comments that AI is more than just a technology. It represents a new kind of intelligence that could lead to:

- Human extinction. If Superintelligence evolves as malicious, humanity may face extinction similar to 99% of other species and several hominids... or
- Human coexistence with Superintelligence. Effective control of AI development could deliver a benevolent Superintelligence, bringing unprecedented prosperity for humanity.

Druzin et al. (2025) argue that, since 'the precaution is a general principle of international law,' international human rights law 'should impose a positive obligation on states under the right to life to proactively take regulatory action to safeguard human life in the face of the possible existential threat posed by machine intelligence.'

References

Acemoglu, D., & Restrepo, P. (2018). The race between man and machine: Implications of technology for growth, factor shares, and employment. *American Economic Review, 108*(6), 1488–1542.

Alabdulatif, A. (2024). Technical and technological solutions towards a sustainable society and circular economy. In J. Mabrouki & A. Mourade (Eds.), *Technical and technological solutions towards a sustainable society and circular economy* (World sustainability series) (pp. 263–277). Springer. https://doi.org/10.1007/978-3-031-56292-1_21

Amnesty International. (2019). *Surveillance giants: How the business model of Google and Facebook threatens human rights.* file:///C:/Users/User/Downloads/POL3014042019ENGLISH.pdf

Autor, D. H. (2015). Why are there still so many jobs? The history and future of workplace automation. *Journal of Economic Perspectives, 29*(3): 3–30.

Barrot, J. (2024). Globalisation and higher education: Integrating generative artificial intelligence into global higher educational systems: Implications for practice, policy, and research. In J. Zajda (Ed.), *Fourth international handbook of globalisation, education and policy research* (pp. 231–250). https://doi.org/10.1007/978-3-031-67667-3_13

Baviera, A. (2025, March 26). *Intelligenza artificiale e geopolitica.* https://www.agensir.it/italia/2025/03/26/intelligenza-artificiale-e-geopolitica-berrettini-un-cattolica-tecnologia-chiave-della-competizione-globale-puo-generare-nuove-asimmetrie-di-potere/

Bendermacher, E., & Moore, M. (2024). *AI in globalization. The next mass extinction or an evolutionary leap?* Multilingual. https://multilingual.com/magazine/march-2024/ai-in-globalization/

Bowles, J. (2014, July 24). *The computerisation of European jobs.* https://www.bruegel.org/blog-post/computerisation-european-jobs

Brekelmans, S., & Petropoulos, G. (2020). *Occupational change, artificial intelligence and the geography of EU labour markets, Bruegel, Stable.* https://www.jstor.org/stable/resrep50101

Capital Economics. (2025). *AI, economies and markets – How artificial intelligence will transform the global economy.* https://www.capitaleconomics.com/ai-economies-and-markets-how-artificial-intelligence-will-transform-global-economy#table-contents

Caruso, C. (2024, August 7). *The risks of artificial intelligence in weapons design.* https://hms.harvard.edu/news/risks-artificial-intelligence-weapons-design

Carvalho, J.-P. (2025, February 14). *The political-economic risks of AI.* https://ssrn.com/abstract=5137622; https://doi.org/10.2139/ssrn.5137622

Cazzaniga, M., Jaumotte, F., Li, L., Melina, G., Panton, A. J., Pizzinelli, C., Rockall, E. J., Mendes Tavares, M. (2024). *Gen-AI: Artificial intelligence and the future of work.* IMF staff discussion notes 2024/001, International Monetary Fund.

Cerutti, E. M., Pascual, A. I. G., Kido, Y., Li, L., Melina, G., Mendes Tavares, M., & Wingender, P. (2025, April 11). *The global impact of AI: Mind the gap.* IMF W. P. 76. https://doi.org/10.5089/9798229008570.001

Cluzel-Metayer, L. (2024, avril 5). *IA: quel potentiel et quels risques dans les services publics?* Vie Publique. https://www.vie-publique.fr/parole-dexpert/293547-ia-quel-potentiel-et-quels-risques-dans-les-services-publics

Cornelli, G., Frost, J., Mishra, S. (2023, October). *Artificial intelligence, services globalisation and income inequality.* BIS working papers no 1135, Monetary and Economic Department.

Czarnecki, T. (2024, November 5). *Do not pause advanced AI development – CONSOLIDATE AI, Sustensis, London.* https://sustensis.co.uk/

Dauvergne, P. (2021, February). The globalization of artificial intelligence: Consequences for the politics of environmentalism. *Globalizations, 2*(18), 285–299. https://doi.org/10.1080/14747731.2020.1785670

Development Aid. (2023, March 22). *How AI can impact developing countries: Positives and negatives.* https://www.developmentaid.org/news-stream/post/158745/how-ai-can-impact-developing-countries

Dias da Silva, A., & Weißler, M. (2025, March 21). AI adoption and employment prospects. *The ECB Blog.* https://www.ecb.europa.eu/press/blog/date/2025/html/ecb.blog20250321~6af1337b6b.en.html

Druzin, B., Boute, A., & Ramsden, M. (2025). Confronting catastrophic risk: The international obligation to regulate artificial intelligence. *Michigan Journal of International Law, 46*(2) https://repository.law.umich.edu/mjil/vol46/iss2/2

Duhienko, N. O., & Sulieimanova, A. N. (2024). Globalization and global trends: Impact of artificial intelligence on the economy. *Financial Strategies of Innovative Economic Development, 59*(3), 54–57.

Engel, C., Linhardt, L., & Schubert, M. (2025). Code is law: How COMPAS affects the way the judiciary handles the risk of recidivism. *Artificial Intelligence and Law, 33,* 383–404. https://doi.org/10.1007/s10506-024-09389-8

Fell, J. (2025). *Stanford just released its annual AI index report. Here's what it reveals.* World Economic Forum. https://www.weforum.org/stories/2024/04/stanford-university-ai-index-report/

Fornes, G., & Altamira, M. (2023). Artificial intelligence and international business. In *Digitalization, technology and global business* (pp. 71–90). Palgrave Pivot. https://doi.org/10.1007/978-3-031-33111-4_5

Francescato, D. (2018, January 4). *Globalization, artificial intelligence, social networks and political polarization: New challenges for community psychologists, community psychology in global perspective, North America.* http://siba-ese.unisalento.it/index.php/cpgp/article/view/17684

Francisco, M. (2023). Artificial intelligence for environmental security: National, international, human and ecological perspectives. *Current Opinion in Environmental Sustainability, 61*(April), 101250. https://doi.org/10.1016/j.cosust.2022.101250

Frank, A. G., Mendes, G. H. S., Ayala, N. F., & Ghezzi, A. (2019). Servitization and industry 4.0 convergence in the digital transformation of product firms: A business model innovation perspective. *Technological Forecasting and Social Change, 141*, 341–351.

Frey, C., & Osborne, M. (2013). *The future of employment: How susceptible are jobs to computerisation?* Working paper, University of Oxford.

Gale, R., & Null, G. (2025, May 31). *The coming artificial intelligence crisis: Power without oversight, global research.* https://www.globalresearch.ca/coming-artificial-intelligence-crisis/5888723

García, S. (2024, June 4). *AI and the globalization of labor markets.* https://www.futureforwork.com/en/ai-and-the-globalization-of-labor-markets/

Georgieff, A., & Hyee, R. (2022). Artificial intelligence and employment: New cross-country evidence. *Frontiers in Artificial Intelligence, 5*, 832736. https://doi.org/10.3389/frai.2022.832736

Georgieva, K. (2024, January 14). AI will transform the global economy. Let's make sure it benefits humanity. *IMF Blog.* https://www.imf.org/en/Blogs/Articles/2024/01/14/ai-will-transform-the-global-economy-lets-make-sure-it-benefits-humanity

Giattino, C., Mathieu, E., Samborska, V., & Roser, M. (2023). *Artificial intelligence.* Published online at OurWorldinData.org. https://ourworldindata.org/artificial-intelligence

Greenbaum, L., Long, F., & Shirley, W. (2023, December 14). *The generative world order: AI, geopolitics, and power.* https://www.goldmansachs.com/insights/articles/the-generative-world-order-ai-geopolitics-and-power

Guarascio, D., & Reljic, J. (2025). AI and employment in Europe. *Economics Letters, 247*(February), 112183. https://doi.org/10.1016/j.econlet.2025.112183

Guryanova, A. V., Shestakov, A. A., & Tikhonov, V. (2021). Digital globalization as a result of the modern economic and technological development. In S. I. Ashmarina, V. V. Mantulenko, M. I. Inozemtsev, & E. L. Sidorenko (Eds.), *Global challenges and prospects of the modern economic development*

(European proceedings of social and behavioural sciences) (Vol. 106, pp. 787–792). European Publisher. https://doi.org/10.15405/epsbs.2021.04.02.94

Hagerty, A., & Rubinov, I. (2019). *Global AI ethics: A review of the social impacts and ethical implications of artificial intelligence*. https://doi.org/10.48550/arXiv.1907.07892

Ilzetzki, E., & Suryaansh, J. (2023, June 20). *The impact of artificial intelligence on growth and employment*. https://cepr.org/voxeu/columns/impact-artificial-intelligence-growth-and-employment

Iqbal, M. S., & Fikri, S. M. (2025). Impact of globalisation, AI adoption, and FinTech integration on banking sector performance and customer satisfaction in post-COVID Pakistan. *The Pakistan Development Review, 64*(1), 1–23.

Kanungo, A. (2023). *The real environmental impact of AI*. https://earth.org/the-green-dilemma-can-ai-fulfil-its-potential-without-harming-the-environment/

Lanzi, D. (2025, January). *Artificial intelligence, development, and stratification economics*. https://doi.org/10.13140/RG.2.2.20639.06569. https://www.researchgate.net/publication/388449295_Artificial_Intelligence_Development_and_Stratification_Economics

Matyushok, V., Krasavina, V., Berezin, A., & Sendra García, J. (2021). The global economy in technological transformation conditions: A review of modern trends. *Economic Research-Ekonomska Istraživanja, 34*(1), 1471–1497. https://doi.org/10.1080/1331677X.2020.1844030

McKinsey & Company Global Institute. (2023, June). *The economic potential of generative AI. The next productivity frontier*. https://www.mckinsey.com/~/media/mckinsey/business%20functions/mckinsey%20digital/our%20insights/the%20economic%20potential%20of%20generative%20ai%20the%20next%20productivity%20frontier/the-economic-potential-of-generative-ai-the-next-productivity-frontier.pdf

Meltzer, J. P. (2018). *The impact of artificial intelligence on international trade*. https://www.brookings.edu/articles/the-impact-of-artificial-intelligence-on-international-trade/

Miguelañez, C. (2025, January 11). *LLM prompt engineering FAQ: Exper, latitude*.https://latitude-blog.ghost.io/blog/llm-prompt-engineering-faq-expert-answers-to-common-questions/

Perlant, C. (2025). Modéliser les épidémies à l'ère de l'intelligence artificielle. *Médecine de Catastrophe Urgences Collectives, 9*(2), 93–95.

Pew Research Center. (2023, July 21). *What shares of workers are most exposed to AI in their jobs?* https://www.pewresearch.org/social-trends/2023/07/26/which-u-s-workers-are-more-exposed-to-ai-on-their-jobs/st_2023-07-26_ai-and-jobs_0-01-png/

Provenzani, F. (2024). *What the world will be like in 2050 according to artificial intelligence, August 18, – Predicting the future is always a challenge, but based on current trends and expectations on technological, social and economic developments.* https://en.money.it/What-the-world-will-be-like-in-2050-according-to-AI

Rana, D. (2022, December 13). The impact of AI on global expansion. *Indian Journal of Law and Legal Research, IV*(VI), 1–21.

Ratten, V. (2024). Artificial intelligence, digital trends and globalization: Future research trends. *FIIB Business Review, 13*(3), 286–293. https://doi.org/10.1177/23197145231222774

Rui, Z., & Bhaumik, A. (2023). A new phase of global streams artificial intelligence and cyber security. *International Journal for Multidisciplinary Research Digital Globalization, 5*(4), 1–11.

Saeed, M., & Sofi, F. (2025, April). Impact of globalisation, AI adoption, and Fintech integration on banking sector performance and customer satisfaction in post-covid Pakistan. *The Pakistan Development Review.* https://doi.org/10.30541/v64i1pp.1-23

Schwab, K. (2017). *The fourth industrial revolution.* Crown Business.

Schwalbe, N., & Wahl, B. (2020). Artificial intelligence and the future of global health. *The Lancet, 395*, 1579–1586. chrome-extension://efaidnbmnnnibpcajpcglclefindmkaj/https://www.thelancet.com/action/showPdf?pii=S0140-6736%2820%2930226-9

Shanmugasundaram, M., & Tamilarasu, A. (2023, November 24). The impact of digital technology, social media, and artificial intelligence on cognitive functions: A review. *Frontiers in Cognition,* Sec. Learning and Cognitive Development, *2.* https://doi.org/10.3389/fcogn.2023.1203077

Shen, Y., & Zhang, X. (2024). The impact of artificial intelligence on employment. The role of virtual agglomeration. *Humanities and Social Sciences Communications, 11*, 122. https://doi.org/10.1057/s41599-024-02647-9

Sichach, M. (2023, September 22). *Technology and globalisation: How social media (narrow artificial intelligence) algorithms and large language models by internet companies have replaced the main stream media as agenda setters for the global culture.* https://ssrn.com/abstract=4580284; https://doi.org/10.2139/ssrn.4580284

Stiglitz, J. E., & Korinek, A. (2025, May 22). The future of inequality: Artificial intelligence, worker-replacing technological progress and income distribution. In *The origins of inequality* (online ed.). Oxford Academic. https://doi.org/10.1093/oso/9780198799580.003.0019

Team GP. (2020, gennaio 16). *L'impatto dell'intelligenza artificiale sull'espansione globale.* https://www.globalization-partners.com/it/blog/the-impact-of-ai-on-global-expansion/

United Nations Regional Information Centre for Western Europe. (2025, April 30). *Artificial intelligence and the future of work: Will AI replace our jobs?* https://unric.org/en/artificial-intelligence-and-the-future-of-work-will-ai-replace-our-jobs/

Vezzoli, M. (2024, February 2). *L'impatto dell'AI nella sfida della globalizzazione.* https://tinnovamag.com/limpatto-dellai-nella-sfida-della-globalizzazione/

Wagner, D. (2018). *How artificial intelligence is changing the global economy, science & technology: Innovation, governance, economics, technology.* https://ourworld.unu.edu/en/how-ai-is-changing-the-global-economy

Wang, Q., Sun, T., & Li, R. (2023). Does artificial intelligence (AI) reduce ecological footprint? The role of globalization. *Environmental Science and Pollution Research, 30*, 123948–123965. https://doi.org/10.1007/s11356-023-31076-5

Weber, S. (2019). *Bloc by Bloc. How to build a global enterprise for the new regional order.* Harvard University Press.

World Bank. (2020). *Artificial intelligence in the public sector. Maximizing opportunities, managing risks.* chrome-extension://efaidnbmnnnibpcajpcglclefindmkaj/, https://documents1.worldbank.org/curated/en/809611616042736565/pdf/Artificial-Intelligence-in-the-Public-Sector-Maximizing-Opportunities-Managing-Risks.pdf

Yudkowsky, E. (2023, March 29). Pausing AI developments isn't enough. We need to shut it all down. *Time.* https://time.com/6266923/ai-eliezer-yudkowsky-open-letter-not-enough/

Zhu, K. (2025, April 27). *Technology visualizing U.S. vs. Chinese AI model performance.* https://www.visualcapitalist.com/visualizing-u-s-vs-chinese-ai-model-performance/

CHAPTER 3

AI and Income Distribution

Abstract Theoretical and empirical work in economics suggest that commercial deployment of AI can amplify the inequality between nations, as the ability to harness AI's benefits theoretical and early empirical work in economics suggest that commercial deployment of advanced AI can impact significantly economic inequality. AI could also widen income disparities within countries, benefitting highly skilled workers, displacing lower-skilled jobs in repetitive tasks, and concentrating wealth among those who control the technology. There is also a third risk, that of AI deployment: 'while AI may fuel within-country inequality, it could also slow or reverse the gains made in reducing between-country inequality. Without targeted policy interventions, AI may deepen the global divide, advancing richer nations while leaving poorer ones further behind, hindering progress towards the Sustainable Development Goals.' AI has a high impact on firms' strategies and life. It can enhance and augment what enterprises can do and is doing things that have never been done before, rather than simply automating or accelerating existing capabilities. Some of the strategic options that emerge won't match past experience or gut feelings.

Keywords Inequality between nations • Income disparities within countries • AI deployment • Impact on firms' strategies and life • Technological unemployment

N. Acocella, *The Economics of Globalization and Artificial Intelligence*, https://doi.org/10.1007/978-3-032-15711-9_3

Vesely and Amaris (2025) note that theoretical and early empirical work in economics suggest that commercial deployment of advanced AI can significantly impact economic inequality, by providing 'the first empirical insights on how may people's preferences for redistribution respond to such AI-induced inequalities.'

According to Schellekens and Skilling (2024), AI could widen income disparities within countries, benefitting highly skilled workers, displacing lower-skilled jobs in repetitive tasks, and concentrating wealth among those who control the technology. At the same time, AI could amplify the inequality between nations, as the ability to harness AI's benefits or mitigate its disruption varies widely across nations. It is true that LDCs have caught up strongly since the late 1980s, leading to absolute convergence between nations since 2000, but more recently there have been erosion of democratic governance and an uneven impact of climate change.

There is also a third risk, that of AI deployment: 'while AI may fuel within-country inequality, it could also slow or reverse the gains made in reducing between-country inequality. Without targeted policy interventions, AI may deepen the global divide, advancing richer nations while leaving poorer ones further behind, hindering progress toward the Sustainable Development Goals.'

In the recent times, the role of AI in social, economic, and environmental decision-making is important. AI is considered to be a source for enabling countries to achieve sustainable development goals (Khan et al., 2025).

Let us first refer to the advantages accruing to innovators. At a micro level, front runners are likely to have a substantial benefit in terms of cash flow and profits. The former can increase a lot in the first years after adoption of the innovation, in contrast with followers, whose gain is very low, and laggards, who lose (see Fig. 3.1).

To the extent to which micro statements can be also applied to a macro level, we could say that innovating countries will obtain large benefits from the innovations they introduce. The only additional problem would be to detect those countries. From the point of view of the conditions for introducing innovations, they can certainly be found in developed countries, but there are certainly outsiders, such as China has been recently.

Liang (2024) says that introduction of AI has had a significant impact on employment, through the automation of routine and repetitive tasks. One effect of this has been job displacement, especially in the manufacturing and administrative sectors, but in other sectors there have been new

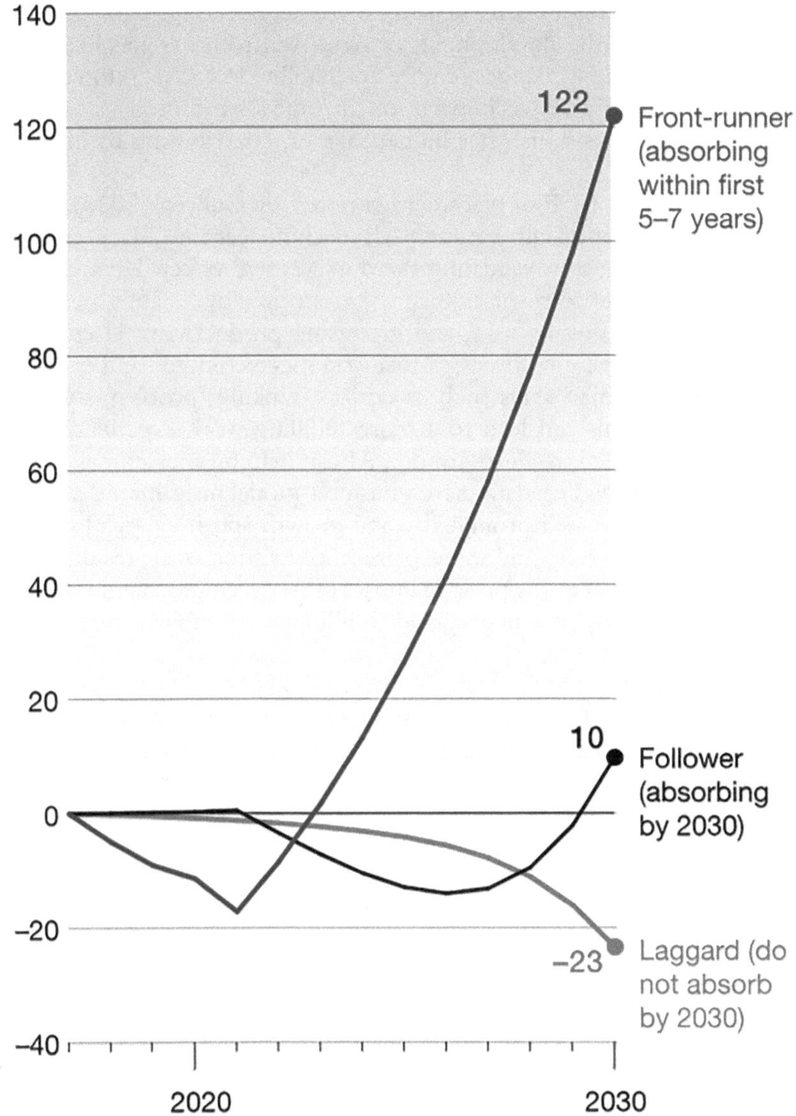

Fig. 3.1 Changes in cash flows deriving from AI adoption (*Source:* Bughin et al., 2018)

employment opportunities, particularly in AI engineering, data science, AI regulation, and the development of AI-driven technologies like self-driving vehicles. These changes require adaptability in the workforce, but also have potential positive impacts on income distribution, 'as high-skilled AI-related positions offer higher salaries, contributing to income inequality.'

A similar effect of job displacement is noted by Guliyev (2023), who finds a negative relationship between AI, machine learning, data science, and unemployment, thus validating the displacement effect. He says that 'AI has the potential to revolutionize the workforce by creating new job roles, automating routine tasks, and increasing productivity. AI-enabled technologies can free employees to focus on more complex and creative work requiring human skills such as critical thinking, problem-solving, and innovation. This can lead to a more fulfilling work experience and increased job satisfaction. Furthermore, AI can help businesses make better decisions by providing data-driven business model insights and analytics, resulting in increased profitability and growth and it can lead to the creation of new job roles and the expansion of existing ones, resulting in job creation. Ultimately, the positive impact of AI on employment is creating a more efficient, productive, and fulfilling work environment with new jobs.'

In contrast with these findings, Gerlich (2024) underscores 'the transformative potential of AI, predicting significant shifts in employment patterns, regulatory challenges, and societal structures.' Specifically, he forecasts a high probability of 'AI-induced unemployment reaching 40–50%, alongside the rapid evolution of AI technologies, outpacing existing governance frameworks, which could exacerbate economic inequalities and societal fragmentation.' The need then arises 'for proactive governance, cross-sector collaboration, and robust regulatory frameworks to ensure that the benefits of technological and geopolitical advancements are harnessed without compromising global stability or societal well-being.'

Wang and Jiao (2025) examine how AI adoption affects labor income share using a comprehensive dataset of 25,156 firm-year observations from Chinese listed companies (2010–2022). They show that 'AI implementation positively influences labor income share through two key channels: improved innovation capacity and accelerated technology upgrading. These effects are more pronounced in nonstate-owned enterprises and nonheavy-polluting industries. These results challenge the conventional narrative of technology-driven labor displacement, suggesting that AI adoption, combined with investments in innovation and human capital, can promote a more equitable distribution of corporate income.'

AI can increase inequality under some conditions, through three main channels: the surplus arising to innovators, redistributions arising from factor price changes, and technological unemployment. Public policy can counter these effects. In fact, under plausible conditions, 'non-distortionary taxation can be levied to compensate those who otherwise might lose. … The proliferation of AI and other forms of worker-replacing technological change can be unambiguously positive in a 1st-best economy in which individuals are fully insured against any adverse effects of innovation, or if it is coupled with the right form of redistribution' (Stiglitz & Korinek, 2025).

Avevor et al. (2023) find that AI adoption has contributed to an increasing concentration of wealth among top income earners, particularly in technology-driven sectors. The 'top 1% of U.S. households experienced a substantial increase in wealth, while the bottom 50% saw only marginal gains, exacerbating the wealth gap.' The key mechanisms driving these disparities include skill-biased technological change and automation, which disproportionately affect low-skilled workers. A need for reskilling initiatives, progressive taxation, and inclusive innovation frameworks arise to ensure that the benefits of AI are equitably distributed.

A similar impact is found by Chen et al. (2024), who find that the application of AI in the service industry significantly reduces the labor income share. 'The main mechanisms of action include the employment structure effect of squeezing out low-educated and frontline workers and the wage-productivity effect that improves labor productivity but benefits capital income, leading to an unequal income distribution.' By improving 'the integration of regional labor markets and workers' bargaining power can help alleviate the negative effects' of AI applications on the share of labor income in the service industry.

Skare et al. (2024), by using an extended Solow–Swan model, and 'conceptualizing AI as a form of capital that can substitute for or complement traditional forms of labor' find 'a positive and statistically significant correlation between AI technology adoption, AI capital stock accumulation, and wealth disparity. The analysis further indicates a complex interaction between income and wealth disparities, suggesting a mutually reinforcing cycle.'

Thus, the proliferation of AI and other forms of worker-replacing technological progress could exacerbate both within-country and between-country inequality, 'thus placing upward pressure on global inequality. High-income individuals and regions benefit disproportionately, while lower-skill workers and resource-poor regions risk being left behind.' Obviously, governments and international organizations can reduce this and other sources of global inequality 'through investments in education, reskilling programs, and social safety nets, progressive taxation and wealth redistribution. International cooperation and targeted aid could support AI adoption in developing countries' (Abbas Khan et al., 2025).

Schellekens and Skilling (2024) note that AI could widen income disparities within countries, benefitting highly skilled workers, displacing lower-skilled jobs in repetitive tasks, and concentrating wealth among those who control the technology. At the same time, AI could amplify the inequality between nations, as the ability to harness AI's benefits or mitigate its disruption varies widely across nations. In fact, wealthy nations can be benefitting much more than others for three reasons:

1. Richer countries are better equipped to harness AI's benefits
2. Poorer countries may be less prepared to handle AI's disruptions
3. AI is intensifying pressure on traditional development models.

'However, AI also holds the potential to reduce inequality—if harnessed for social good.' AI-driven innovations in healthcare, education, and agriculture can uplift living standards in developing countries, closing the gap between the rich and the poor. For instance, precision farming powered by AI can boost crop yields for smallholder farmers, while AI-enabled education tools can bring quality learning to remote areas (Schellekens & Skilling, 2024).

In the case of possible adverse labor market impacts of AI, which has led to widespread anxiety, innovative efforts can to some extent be steered so as to increase labor demand and create better-paying jobs. This requires 'to identify the properties that make an innovation desirable from the perspective of workers, including its technological complementarity to labor, the factor share of labor in producing the goods involved, and the relative income of the affected workers.' Steering technology 'becomes more desirable the less efficient social safety nets are. If technological progress devalues labor, the desirability of steering is at first increased, but beyond a critical threshold, it becomes less effective, and policy should shift toward greater redistribution. If labor's economic value diminishes in the future, progress should increasingly focus on enhancing human well-being rather than labor productivity' (Korinek & Stiglitz, 2025).

This technological inequality between advanced and developing countries depends on five factors: (a) investment in development and implementation of AI; (b) overall nation capacity to innovate AI; (c) infrastructure of (IoT)/AI; (d) nation policy to the adoption of AI technology, and (e) technology barriers between countries. Technology barriers mean that time lags behind to give (deliver) new/advanced technology from one nation to another.

AI has largely increased technological disparities between countries, which has led to advanced countries becoming more sophisticated in technology and lagging countries adopting advanced technology. Countries like India want to make full use of AI; and India is increasing investment in AI (Kumar et al., 2018). Because of this, a distinction develops between developed and developing nations to adopting the technology.

The uneven adoption of AI technologies causes a deepening of 'the economic divide between countries, as developed countries benefit from advanced infrastructure while developing and underdeveloped countries lag behind.' Solutions such as retraining programs, redistributing tax systems of income deriving from AI technologies, and international cooperation to ensure equal access to AI opportunities, are necessary (Abduvaliev, 2024).

Figure 3.2 shows that females are always more exposed to AI, being either high complementary or not.

Figure 3.3 shows, instead, that high exposure associated to low complementarity do not vary too much as between low and high deciles, whereas high exposure associated to high complementarity rise passing from low to high deciles.

Menzies et al. (2024) explore AI's potential in a number of international business strategies, practices, and activities, such as international market selection, entry modes, foreign exchange, and international supply chains, indicating managerial implications, and suggesting areas requiring future studies.

As to the geographic impact of AI, we can say that Europe tends to fall behind the United States and China for developing and applying AI for three reasons: (1) the first is the European Union's relative underfunding of basic research; (2) in addition, 'it lags in computing power to support research'; (3) finally, the 'failure to fully leverage the large scale of the

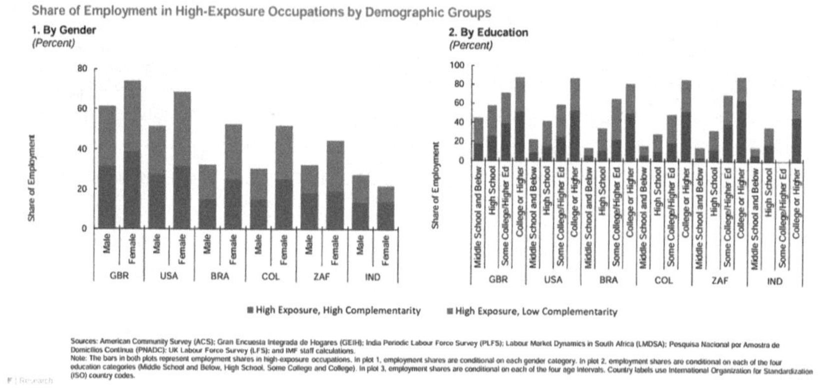

Fig. 3.2 Share of people employed in highly exposed jobs, by sex and education. (*Source:* Cazzaniga et al., 2024). *Note:* The lower part of histograms indicates: High exposure, high complementarity. The higher part: High exposure, low complementarity. The countries are: GBR, USA, Brazil, Colombia, South Africa (ZAF), Indonesia

European economy,' as 'scale is a huge advantage in determining return on investment'; a large scale is not obtained since 'European capital markets remain fragmented; service market integration is incomplete and hampered by fragmented regulation at the national level. China is an AI powerhouse. India, with its strong roots in digital technology, a large and growing internal market, and deep reservoirs of engineering human capital, is likely to be a growing force. The rest of the emerging market economies may benefit greatly from AI applications, but for the next few years at least, they will be largely consumers of advanced AI technology generated mostly in the US and China' (Spence, 2024).

Building a large AI industry will likely increase the country's trade surplus with the rest of the world, particularly in services. Skilled foreign workers will for the first time be exposed to competition from a low-wage country. In isolation, this would reduce one dimension of domestic US inequality. If the Chinese market becomes open to US technology giants (and vice versa), both the Melitz (2003) model and the Argente et al. (2021) model of trade predict that the giants will grow even larger. In the context in which these companies have already absorbed one fifth of US value added, and may have contributed to US top-end inequality, the

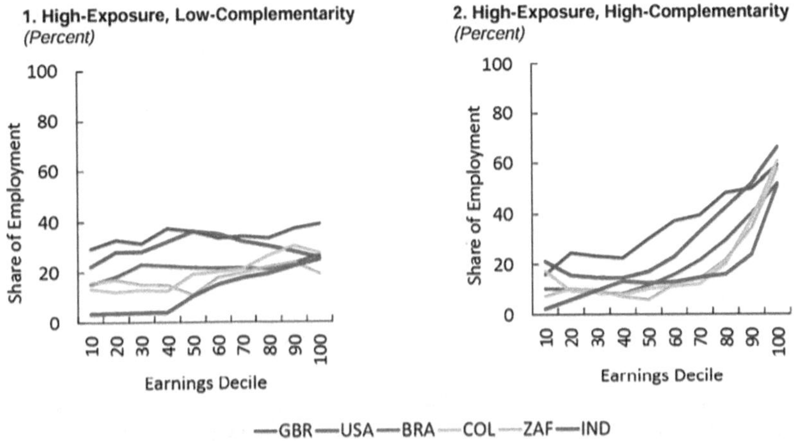

Fig. 3.3 Share of employment in high-exposure occupations and potential complementarity by income deciles (*Source:* Cazzaniga et al., 2024). *Note:* In panel 1, for the third decile from the top, countries are: GBR, USA, Brazil, Colombia, South Africa (ZAF), Indonesia. In panel 2, for the first decile, from the top countries are: USA, Colombia, GBR, Brazil, South Africa (ZAF), Indonesia

impact of international trade in further growing these impacts may increase top-end inequality.

AI has a high impact on firms' strategies and life. It 'can enhance and augment what enterprises can do and is doing things that have never been done before, rather than simply automating or accelerating existing capabilities. Some of the strategic options that emerge won't match past experience or gut feelings.' (PWC, n.d.).

The nature of the technology suggests that economies of scale and scope are important. Furthermore, as a knowledge-intensive industry, knowledge externalities are likely to be important. Prior literature on other industries suggests that such externalities are often local, but more evidence is needed. Second, the trade models that are likely to be most useful in understanding the impact of AI are those that account for these points, specifically, scale, knowledge creation, and the geography of knowledge diffusion. These models suggest that whether AI-focused trade policies (or AI-focused investments in clusters) are optimal will depend very much on the presence of scale and the absence of rapid international knowledge diffusion. Third, we discussed whether and how regulation might be used to favor domestic industry. We highlighted that privacy policy targeting consumer protection is unlike many other regulations in that it is likely to hamstring domestic firms, even relative to foreign ones. So, rather than focusing trade discussions on how privacy policy might be used as a disguised restriction on trade, such discussions should emphasize regulatory harmonization so as to avoid a race to the bottom. In contrast, several other policies may be used to favor domestic firms including data localization rules, limited access to government data, industry regulations such as those around the use of drones, and forced access to source code. Generally, this is an exciting new area for trade research and policy. There is still much to learn before we have a comprehensive understanding of these questions.

As to the various topics, the general effects of AI are the object of Furman and Seamans (2019), who note that AI is having a large effect on the economy. In fact, AI and robotics have the potential to increase productivity growth but may have mixed effects on labor, particularly in the short run.

As to the effects of AI on wages, Gries and Naudé (2020) find that: (a) AI automation can decrease the share of labor income no matter the size of the elasticity of substitution between AI and labor, and (b) when this elasticity is high, AI will unambiguously reduce aggregate demand and slow down GDP growth, even in the face of the positive technology shock that AI entails. If the elasticity of substitution is low, then GDP, productivity, and wage growth may however still slow down, because the economy will then fail to benefit from the supply side driven capacity expansion potential that AI can deliver. If the progress in AI is significant and the elasticity of substitution between labor and AI high enough, the effect of AI to increase inequality and reduce demand becomes dominant.

AI can have an effect of job displacement and raise unemployment. In fact, Liang Y. (2024) analyzes job displacement, the emergence of new roles, and the widening income gap between high- and low-income groups. They note that the phenomenon of the integration of AI into industries resulting in job displacement is not solely marked by job losses. AI has also brought about job transformation, necessitating individuals to acquire new skill sets and collaborate effectively with AI systems, paved the way for new employment opportunities particularly in AI engineering, data science, AI regulation, and the development of AI-driven technologies like self-driving vehicles.

Goyal and Aneja (2020) conclude that AI has led to mass unemployment and various types of inequalities in the recent years. Income inequality has increased with the changes in technology.

The study finds that the relationship between AI and income distribution has always been considered negative and this is what they observe in their study, which directly affects the distribution of income and jobs.

Wang et al. (2023) find that AI has a U-shaped effect on the distribution of income between profits and wages (see Fig. 3.4). The effect of AI on the distribution of income between profits and wages is heterogeneous across enterprises, entrepreneurs, and industries.

When the number of AI patents in the province is in the range of [0, 87.0], AI will narrow the gap between profits and wages. In the interval (87.0, +∞), AI will induce profits to erode wages.

According to Wang and Jiao (2025) the increased use of AI will lead to greater income inequality and a more polarized society concerns around AI's potential to exacerbate income inequality. High-income workers

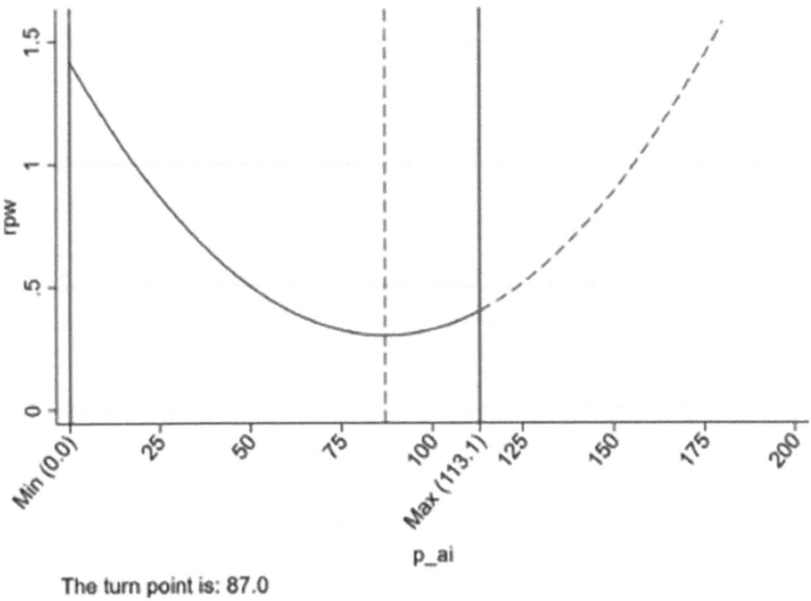

Fig. 3.4 U-shaped relationship between AI shocks from the province level and the ratio of profits to wages. (*Source:* Wang et al., 2023)

appear most likely to benefit from AI-driven productivity boosts in the near term.

A 2023 survey of thousands of leading AI researchers from academia and industry put the probability of all human occupations being fully automatable at 10% by 2037 and over 50% within the next century.

Avevor (2023) notes that AI adoption has contributed to an increasing concentration of wealth among top income earners, particularly in technology-driven sectors. The analysis reveals that the top 1% of US households experienced a substantial increase in wealth, while the bottom 50% saw only marginal gains, exacerbating the wealth gap.

Key mechanisms are driving these disparities, including skill-biased technological change and automation, which disproportionately affect low-skilled workers.

Implications for policy suggest a need for reskilling initiatives, progressive taxation, and inclusive innovation frameworks to ensure that the benefits of AI are equitably distributed. This research highlights the urgent need for targeted interventions to mitigate the adverse effects of technological advancements on wealth.

According to Challoumis (2024) the rise of AI enhances productivity but also raises pivotal questions about job displacement and wealth inequality.

For Dizikes (2022), over the last four decades, the income gap between more- and less-educated workers has grown significantly. He finds that automation accounts for more than half of that increase.

As to the rise in income inequalities across countries Freire (2025) examines the impact of AI in countries at different levels of income using computer simulations of a multi-country multi-sector macroeconomic model. AI results in only small changes at the aggregated level of GDP and employment. However, it increases income inequality across countries. AI also results in considerable shifts in jobs between production sectors and R&D. AI has an impact on the GDP and employment in low-, middle-, and high-income countries, as well as on the income inequality across countries.

Introduction of AI results in only small changes at the aggregated level of GDP and employment. However, there is an increase in income inequality across countries, and there are considerable shifts in jobs between production sectors and R&D.

AI may not cause mass technological unemployment, but would still result in large distributional changes in low-, middle-, and high-income countries.

Income inequalities tend to rise in the long run. Liu and Liang (2025) overlooked the influence of AI on wealth distribution. There is a temporal dichotomy in AI's effects on wealth inequality: in the short term, AI exacerbates disparities in wealth distribution, while the long-term outcomes depend on the extent of AI's influence across different technological domains. They suggest policy recommendations for China to leverage AI for economic growth while mitigating inequality.

Skare et al. (2024) reveal a significant correlation between AI adoption and wealth disparity, providing insights for policy-making and corporate strategy. The study fills a significant gap in the existing literature by offering a novel perspective on the distributional impact of AI.

Sholler and MacInnes (2024) first ask which policies and technologies can reduce income inequality in the presence of AI. 'They conclude that the increasing capabilities of AI demand require a more active approach. This can include union activity and policies related to universal basic income, wage subsidies, unemployment, reskilling initiatives, rewards for workers that are improving AI, and addressing remote work. A key goal would be to increase the bargaining power of workers.'

Solos and Leonard (2022) focus their analysis 'on the promotion of AI on productivity and economic growth; the impact of AI on labor employment; and the question of whether AI will increase income inequality.' They then suggest how to implement public policies to reduce the potential negative impacts of AI on the employment structure and income inequality.

Lowitzsch and Magalhães (2025) argue that to offset the disadvantages of AI/automation and further capital concentration, all citizens should be enabled to (co-)own technology and benefit from the second income source capital ownership provides.

Ghosh et al. (2025) detail out the fundamental inferences drawn by the recent literature on AI-enabled economic repercussions, deciphering 'the skill types that possibly would see the largest impacts, the sectors that might see plethora of, whether indeed there will be an overall net job destruction or net-job creation,' and how they differ across economic regions.

References

Abbas Khan, M., Khan, H., Omer, M. F., Ullah, I., & Yasir, M. (2025). Impact of artificial intelligence on the global economy and technology advancements. In S. El Hajjami, K. Kaushik, & I. U. Khan (Eds.), *Artificial General Intelligence (AGI) security. Advanced technologies and societal change*. Springer. https://doi.org/10.1007/978-981-97-3222-7_7

Abduvaliev, A. (2024). The economic implications of AI on income distribution and global inequality. *Journal of New Century Innovations, 66*(1), 60–65. https://scientific-jl.org/index.php/new

Argente, D., Moreira, S., Oberfield, E., & Venkateswaran, V. (2021, July 2). *Scalable expertise*, W. P., 4.

Avevor, M., Tawo, O. E., Akinola, O. A., Osahor, D., Awofadeju, M., & Azonuche, T. (2023). AI and technology's influence on economic inequality: A study of wealth distribution in the U.S. *World Journal of Advanced Research and Reviews, 19*(01), 1607–1617.

Bughin, J., Seong, J., Manyika, J., Chui, M., & Joshi, R. (2018). *Notes from the AI frontier: Modeling the impact of AI on the world economy, September 4, Discussion paper.* https://www.mckinsey.com/featured-insights/artificial-intelligence/notes-from-the-AI-frontier-modeling-the-impact-of-ai-on-the-world-economy

Cazzaniga, M., Jaumotte, F., Li, L., Melina, G., Panton, A. J., Pizzinelli, C., Rockall, E. J., Mendes Tavares, M. (2024). *Gen-AI: Artificial intelligence and the future of work.* IMF staff discussion notes 2024/001, International Monetary Fund.

Challoumis, C. (2024, November 15). *AI and the economy – How technology is redefining employment and income distribution*, MPRA.

Chen, Z., Chen, C., Yang, G., He, X., Chi, X., Zeng, Z. & Chen, X. (2024, July 5). Research integrity in the era of artificial intelligence: Challenges and responses. *Medicine (Baltimore), 103*(27), e38811. https://doi.org/10.1097/MD.0000000000038811. PMID: 38968491; PMCID: PMC11224801

Dizikes, P. (2022, November 21). Automation drives income inequality. *MIT News*. https://doi.org/10.35631/AIJBES.619012

Freire, C. (2025). Is this time different? Impact of AI in output, employment and inequality across low, middle and high-income countries. *Structural Change and Economic Dynamics, 73*, 136–157.

Furman, J., & Seamans, R. (2019). AI and the economy. *Innovation Policy and the Economy, 19*, 161–191. https://doi.org/10.1086/699936

Gerlich, M. (2024). Brace for impact: Facing the AI revolution and geopolitical shifts in a future societal scenario for 2025–2040. *Societies, 14*(9), 180. https://doi.org/10.3390/soc14090180

Ghosh, D., Ghosh, R., Chowdhury, S. R., & Ganguly, B. (2025). AI-exposure and labour market: A systematic literature review on estimations, validations, and perceptions. *Management Review Quarterly, 2025*(75), 677–704. https://doi.org/10.1007/s11301-023-00393-x

Goyal, A., & Aneja, R. (2020). Artificial intelligence and income inequality: Do technological changes and worker's position matter? *Journal of Public Affairs*, 02 September. https://doi.org/10.1002/pa.2326

Gries, Th., & Naudé, W. (2020). Artificial Intelligence, income distribution and economic growth, GLO Discussion Paper Series 632, Global Labor Organization (GLO).

Guliyev, H. (2023). Artificial intelligence and unemployment in high-tech developed countries: New insights from dynamic panel data model. *Research in Globalization, 7*, 100140. www.sciencedirect.com/journal/research-in-globalization

Khan, M. W., Destek, M. A., & Khan, Z. (2025). Income inequality and artificial intelligence: Globalization and age dependency for developed countries. *Social Indicators Research: An International and Interdisciplinary Journal for Quality-of-Life Measurement, 176*(3), 1207–1233.

Korinek, A., & Stiglitz, J. (2025, May 5). *Steering technological progress.* INET W. P. No. 232.

Kumar, D., Jain, R., & Deb, V. (2018). Artificial Intelligence. Creating automated insights for customer relationship management, January, https://doi.org/10.1109/CONFLUENCE.2018.8442900, 8th International Conference on Cloud Computing, Data Science & Engineering (Confluence).

Liang, Y. (2024, March, 27). The impact of artificial intelligence on employment and income distribution. *Journal of Education Humanities and Social Sciences*, 166–171. https://doi.org/10.54097/2a7a8830

Liu, F., & Liang, C. (2025). Analyzing wealth distribution effects of artificial intelligence: A dynamic stochastic general equilibrium approach. *Heliyon*, 11.

Lowitzsch, J., & Magalhães, R. (2025). Automation, artificial intelligence and capital concentration – A race for the machine. *International Review of Applied Economics, 39*(2–3), 197–215.

Melitz, M. (2003). The impact of trade on aggregate industry productivity and intra-industry reallocations. *Econometrica, 71*(6), 16951725.

Menzies, J., Sabert, B., Hassan, R., & Kofi Mensah, P. (2024). Artificial intelligence for international business: Its use, challenges, and suggestions for future research and practice. *Thunderbird International Business Review*. https://doi.org/10.1002/tie.22370

PWC. (n.d.). *Sizing the prize. What's the real value of AI for your business and how can you capitalise?* chrome-extension://efaidnbmnnnibpcajpcglclefindmkaj/, https://www.pwc.com/gx/en/issues/analytics/assets/pwc-ai-analysis-sizing-the-prize-report.pdf

Schellekens, Ph., & Skilling, D. (2024, October 17). *Three reasons why AI may widen global inequality.* Center for Global Development. https://www.cgdev.org/blog/three-reasons-why-ai-may-widen-global-inequality

Sholler, D., & MacInnes, I. (2024). AI and income inequality: The danger of exacerbating existing trends toward polarization in the US workforce. In M. Garcia-Murillo, I. MacInnes, & A. Renda (Eds.), *Chapter 17 of Handbook of artificial intelligence at work* (pp. 338–355). Elgar. https://doi.org/10.4337/9781800889972.000

Skare, M., Gavurova, B., & Blažević Burić, S. (2024). Artificial intelligence and wealth inequality: A comprehensive empirical exploration of socioeconomic implications. *Technology in Society, 79*, 102719.

Solos, W. K., & Leonard, J. (2022). On the impact of artificial intelligence on economy. *Science Insights, 41*(1), 501–560.

Spence, M. (2024). *AI's promise for the global economy*. https://www.imf.org/en/Publications/fandd/issues/2024/09/AIs-promise-for-the-global-economy-Michael-Spence#:~:text=With%20policy%20support,aggressively%20but%20wisely

Stiglitz, J. E., & Korinek, A. (2025, May 22). The future of inequality: Artificial intelligence, worker-replacing technological progress and income distribution. In *The origins of inequality* (online ed.). Oxford Academic. https://doi.org/10.1093/oso/9780198799580.003.0019

Vesely, S., & Amaris, G. (2025). AI-driven income inequality and preferences for redistribution. *Economic Analysis and Policy, Qeios*. https://doi.org/10.32388/7HWUZ2

Wang, C., & Jiao, D. (2025). Impact of artificial intelligence on the labor income distribution: Labor substitution or production upgrading? *Finance Research Letters, 73*(C) Elsevier.

Wang, Q., Sun, T., & Li, R. (2023). Does artificial intelligence (AI) reduce ecological footprint? The role of globalization. *Environmental Science and Pollution Research, 30*, 123948–123965. https://doi.org/10.1007/s11356-023-31076-5

CHAPTER 4

AI and Foreign Trade

Abstract The development of AI-supporting devices such as computer chips or semiconductors is a result of globalization and the global supply chain. Now we are in a phase of de-globalization. De-globalization can be seen from the U.S. trade wars with China.

> Governments around the world are freely spending public funds on new AI clusters designed to shift international comparative advantage towards their favoured regions.

AI affects the pattern of trade through economies of scale and scope and knowledge externalities.

AI's practical applications have significant benefits, even if the adoption of AI in international trade is not without challenges (data quality, ethical concerns, technological complexity, and public perception). To be noted is the transformative impact of AI on international trade and its specific applications in areas such as data analytics and translation services, which are reducing barriers to trade.

Policy recommendations highlight the need for a robust data infrastructure, establishing ethical AI guidelines, fostering international cooperation to align data protection regulations.

N. Acocella, *The Economics of Globalization and Artificial Intelligence*, https://doi.org/10.1007/978-3-032-15711-9_4

Keywords AI-supporting devices • Global supply chain • De-globalization • AI clusters • Economies of scale and scope • Knowledge externalities • AI's practical applications • Policy recommendations

> Currently, the U.S. dominates the AI landscape, scoring 70.06 on Stanford's 2023 AI Index, while China lags at 40.17. This rivalry sets the stage for a technological race that hints at potential de-globalization. (O'Connor, 2025)

Setiawan (2025) correctly notes that 'the development of AI itself cannot be separated from globalization. More specifically, the development of AI-supporting devices such as computer chips or semiconductors is a result of globalization and the global supply chain.' Now we are in a phase of de-globalization, that is, with a series of attempts to make a world less connected conducted by powerful nation-states, by stricter trade restrictions and protectionist policies such as tariffs, local content requirements, and inward investment. These derive 'from nationalist-centered foreign policies, the rise of populism, or international crises where states tend to help themselves first.' De-globalization can be seen from the 2018 US trade war with China, the United States Innovation and Competition Act of 2021, the enactment of a new export control of semiconductors to China in October 2022 by the United States, and similar actions of October 2023, December 2024, and March 2025. These actions have caused a major blow to the American companies, because of the ensuing drop in their world market shares. Setiawan comments: 'What makes it funny is that the development of technology and AI was boosted by globalization with cross-border cooperation from many individuals and experts. However, the existence of AI turns out to be the antithesis of globalization, which is de-globalization.'

Goldfarb and Trefler (2018) argue that 'governments around the world are freely spending public funds on new AI clusters designed to shift international comparative advantage towards their favored regions.' It is important to understand the international dimensions of AI innovations and policies. AI affects the pattern of trade through economies of scale and scope and knowledge externalities. Whether AI-focused trade policies (or AI-focused investments in clusters) are optimal will depend very much on the presence of scale and the absence of rapid international knowledge diffusion. In order to avoid a race to the bottom deriving from competitive policy actions by different countries. In contrast, 'several other policies may be used to favor domestic firms including data localization rules, limited access to government data, industry regulations such as those around the use of drones, and forced access to source code.'

Ferencz et al. (2022) note that, 'while AI technologies have the potential to fundamentally change trade and international business models, trade itself can also be an important mechanism through which countries and firms access the inputs needed to build AI systems, whether goods, services, people or data, and through which they can deploy AI solutions globally.' In fact, AI has offered the possibility to automate cognitive tasks by using complex algorithms and data to make predictions. The applications of this to international trade have been numerous. They have interest in productivity improvements, efficiency gains along supply chains, and reductions in trade costs. Indeed, evidence highlights that AI innovations are particularly important in highly tradable sectors, including ICT goods and services.

Ferencz et al also underscore 'the importance of trade in goods, trade in services, as well as the movement of human expertise and data as essential ingredients for enabling AI.' They also note that 'barriers on goods, services, people and data remain, affecting the deployment of AI solutions. For instance, many countries, particularly developing and emerging economies, still have tariffs on ICT goods.'

Kulesz (2024) underlines the profound transformation of multiple dimensions of international cultural relations derived from the integration of AI systems. 'Notably, changes in recent years have accentuated imbalances among languages, affected the situation of cultural sectors, and impacted the integrity of information while also providing a platform for influential tech players with unique imaginaries. This is unfolding in an era characterised by an increasing geopolitical competition and a global search for new AI governance frameworks. Most of these issues will likely further intensify in the coming years, with the proliferation of AI agents with whom users will interact in various contexts.' In such a scenario, it has become urgent to outline a strategy for the work in the field of these international cultural relations in the AI era. Considering the mutual influence between AI and these relations, institutions engaged in them should aim to ensure ethical and responsible technology use and emerge as pivotal contributors to the advancement and regulation of AI.

Ozturk (2024) explores the transformative potential of AI in international trade, focusing on its key roles in optimizing trade operations (e.g., by enhancing trade finance and expanding market access) and customs procedures, automating trade finance and enhancing transactional transparency, particularly through integration with blockchain technology. Also market access can benefit from AI by the possibility to identify consumer trends and competitive dynamics, enabling personalized marketing and overcoming linguistic and cultural barriers.

In trade finance, AI can automate document processing and risk assessment, increasing access to finance and enhancing transactional transparency, particularly through integration with blockchain technology. In terms of market access, AI-driven analytics can identify consumer trends and competitive dynamics, enabling personalized marketing and overcoming linguistic and cultural barriers. Due to the lack of quantitative data, this study employed qualitative research methods, specifically a multiple-case-study approach. The case studies of leading companies such as Alibaba, DHL, and Maersk showcase how they leverage AI to optimize their trade operations, improve customer service, and achieve greater efficiency. These real-world examples demonstrate AI's practical applications and significant benefits in the global trade landscape. However, the adoption of AI in international trade is not without challenges. These include issues around data quality, ethical concerns, technological complexity, and public perception. Policy recommendations highlight the need for a robust data infrastructure, establishing ethical AI guidelines, and fostering international cooperation to align data protection regulations.

Meltzer (2018) notes the transformative impact of AI on international trade and its specific applications in areas such as data analytics and translation services. 'These applications are reducing barriers to trade. In fact, international trade rules can address challenges in the development of AI such as improving global access to data to train AI systems. AI stands to have a transformative impact on international trade. Already, specific applications in areas such as data analytics and translation services are reducing barriers to trade.' At the same time, some challenges in the development of AI that international trade rules can be addressed. One of them is improving global access to data to train AI systems. The paper provides an overview of some of the key AI opportunities for trade.

The World Economic Forum (2024a) deals with the way in which the emerging technology ChatWTO is transforming global trade. This is done by enhancing productivity, streamlining supply chains, and creating new opportunities for cross-border transactions. The paper examines both the potential benefits and the challenges generative AI poses, such as regulatory hurdles, data privacy concerns, and intellectual property issues.

Meltzer (2024) first clarifies that 'foundational' AI is a general-purpose technology that will affect economic activity across industries, as it 'has potentially significant impacts on jobs and international trade, due to automation of routine and nonroutine white-collar jobs, which reduces international trade where these jobs are on-shored,' possibly opening up new opportunities for international trade in services. Its effects on international trade also depend on how it is regulated, which is an increasing focus in free trade agreements and digital economy agreements.

Rashid and Kausik (2024) deal with the various AI technologies—machine learning, deep learning, robotics, big data, the Internet of Things, natural language processing, image processing, object detection, virtual reality, augmented reality, speech recognition, and computer vision—that have nowadays a number of applications in many industries, ranging from agriculture to education, autonomous systems, healthcare, finance, entertainment, transportation, military, manufacturing, etc. The paper thus practically explores the immense potential of AI technology.

AI has been integrated into various sectors, including commerce, advertising, and finance. There have been developments in the tech industry that have seen a significant push toward the integration of Visa Intelligent Commerce, Mastercard and PayPal, Met, Apple, Galaxefi, Allvue Systems, and Anthropic sa AI Commerce, Meta AI Returns, Apple AI Demand, Galaxefi Foreign Trade, Nvidia AI Chip Policy (https://thejoai.com/ai-news/visa-ai-commerce-meta-ai-returns-apple-ai-demand-galaxefi-foreign-trade-nvidia-ai-chip-policy/).

Cui (2025) investigates the impact of AI technology on cross-border trade using a qualitative content analysis approach. It synthesizes existing empirical studies, aiming to quantify the overall effect of AI on trade flows and identify the key moderating and mediating variables. AI adoption significantly increases trade volumes in Southeast Asia. Likewise, more in regions with advanced technological infrastructure and favorable regulatory frameworks. In addition, 'trade firm size partially mediates the relationship between AI technology and trade performance.' Furthermore, this study draws on several key theoretical frameworks—such as those on technology, organization, and environment, that on the diffuse innovation theory, the dynamic capabilities theory and others—'that provide a comprehensive understanding of the mechanisms through which AI technology is affecting cross-border trade in Southeast Asia.'

Piao (2024) analyzes 'the unique advantages of AI in enhancing trade efficiency and optimizing trade structures,' by dissecting the internal driving forces and the external factors that facilitate its development. The paper explores both the benefits and challenges of integrating AI into international trade and offers various kinds of guidance for newcomers in the foreign trade industry.

SalesAI (2025) refers to the integration of AI technologies into foreign trade processes, enabling businesses to automate repetitive tasks, analyze large datasets, and optimize operations. The paper delves into the benefits and applications of AI in trade automation, offering insights on how businesses can adopt these technologies to stay competitive. By utilizing AI, companies can: identify high-potential leads faster; automate marketing campaigns across multiple platforms; track and analyze trade data for actionable insights.

> These capabilities make AI a valuable asset for businesses looking to streamline their workflows and achieve measurable growth in the global market. AI-powered trade automation is reshaping the foreign trade industry by providing innovative solutions to long-standing challenges. From lead generation to marketing automation, businesses can now leverage AI tools to enhance efficiency, reduce costs, and improve their global reach.

Yin et al. (2024) study the complex impact mechanism of AI technology on international trade. This provides an answer to how different countries use AI technology to increase their own international trade volume. This article is based on an analysis of cross-sectional data for 139 countries in 2021. This paper uses the OLS method to perform an analysis on the cross-sectional data. This paper finds that the membership of WTO has obvious significance for a country to use AI technology to promote exports. In countries with a high Government AI Readiness Index, AI technology has a significant role in promoting the growth of international trade. However, there is a significant negative correlation between the number of patent applications for AI-related technologies, and imports and exports across countries. Besides, the number of patent applications for AI-related technology has increased through time.

> The future of AI holds tremendous promise for transforming our world. While we have witnessed significant advancements in AI, there are still challenges to overcome, including ethical considerations and potential job displacement. However, with careful planning, collaboration, and ethical frameworks, we can harness the power of AI to revolutionize industries, enhance personalized experiences, and drive advancements in sectors such as healthcare, finance, and transportation.

A number of advantages can derive from international trade, going from the provision of significant efficiencies in managing and processing data related to trade flows and customs, which can: enable businesses to reduce costs, improve accuracy, and speed up processes; enhance risk management in international trade, helping businesses to identify potential risks and take appropriate action to mitigate them; provide valuable insights and intelligence for businesses operating in international markets, helping them to better understand consumer preferences and market trends; result in a more efficient, effective, and dynamic global trading system, with improved business outcomes, greater consumer satisfaction, and increased economic growth.

AI does not offer only potential benefits in international trade, but also several concerns and challenges, such as job displacement and income inequality, as businesses may shift to automated processes in order to reduce costs, the risk of bias and discrimination in AI algorithms, which can perpetuate existing inequalities and exacerbate social and economic divisions, and the lack of transparency and accountability in decision-making processes, which can be 'particularly problematic in areas such as trade policy and regulation, where transparency and accountability are crucial for fair and effective decision-making.' There is also the possibility of a wrong choice of technology, that of a concentration of power, the risk of AI development being dominated by a small number of large corporations and governments could exacerbate inequality and limit diversity in AI applications (Marr, 2023).

From enabling small firms to compete globally to making supply chains more sustainable,

AI's impact extends far beyond efficiency gains. A report examines both how AI is currently being used in trade and the choices that will define its future effects:

1. Will AI help or hinder international trade?
2. How ai-for-foreign-trade-enhances-efficiency-and-business-growth
3. How to use AI in Foreign sales.

It's now likely that 2023 will mark a critical inflection point for AI, after certain watershed years such as, that for internet usage (exploded with the popularity of the browser in 1995), and the smartphone growth, which accelerated in 2007 with the launch of the iPhone. 'We need to use this watershed year not just to launch new AI advances, but to responsibly and effectively address both the promises and perils that lie ahead. The stakes are high. AI may well represent the most consequential technology advance of our lifetime. And while that's saying a lot, there's good reason to say it. Today's cutting-edge AI is a powerful tool for advancing critical thinking and stimulating creative expression. It makes it possible not only to search for information but to seek answers to questions. It can help people uncover insights amid complex data and processes. It speeds up our ability to express what we learn more quickly. Perhaps most important, it's going to do all these things better and better in the coming months and years.'

Ganne et al. (2024) examine the relationships between AI and international trade. They highlight AI's 'potential to transform global trade patterns by reducing trade costs, enhancing productivity, and reshaping comparative advantages.' Also policy considerations are discussed, 'including the risk of regulatory fragmentation and the importance of global cooperation to promote and regulate AI.' The analysis underscores the WTO's critical role in facilitating AI-related trade, ensuring trustworthy AI, and addressing emerging trade tensions.

The emergence of consumer-facing generative AI tools has radically shifted public conversation around the power and potential of AI. 'The impact of generative AI on economies and enterprise will be revolutionary.' McKinsey Global Institute estimates that generative AI will add between \$2.6 and \$4.4 trillion in annual value to the global economy, increasing the economic impact of AI as a whole by 15–40%.

AI raises concerns over the national security, safety, and privacy implications. States have imposed restrictions on data transfer, utilized automated decision-making, mandated algorithmic transparency, and limited market access.

'Restrictions on data transfer, mandates for algorithmic transparency, automated decision-making, and limitations on market access are, to varying degrees, barriers to foreign investment' are in some instances, rational regulatory responses to the public policy issues deriving from AI. The international investment regime provides an unpredictable legal environment in which to adjudicate the emerging norms and ethics of AI.

Several reforms can mitigate the uncertainty deriving from current norms. One of those reforms would require treaty standards to be drafted with more precision to reinforce their anti-protectionist purpose.

In the foreign trade industry AI is largely applied, in terms not only of technological innovation to the foreign trade industry, but also as a profound change in the business model, through: customer data analysis, automated business communication improving work efficiency; market trend forecasting that seize business opportunity in advance; intelligent translation and localization; supply chain optimization; smart contracts and payments. 'Foreign trade personnel can greatly improve work efficiency, reduce operating costs, enhance customer experience, and ultimately occupy a favorable position in the fiercely competitive international market.'

According to World Economic Forum (2025), the following four factors can increase the ease of AI implementation in trade:

1. ensuring system interoperability;
2. building trust;
3. facilitating public-private partnerships (PPPs) to align incentives;
4. investing in workforce development and digital infrastructure to strengthen human AI collaboration.

Achieving both rapid innovation and inclusive participation requires extensive collaboration and coordination across all parties in the trade ecosystem. Thankfully, AI can facilitate just that.

A global value chain (GVC) is a supply chain crossing international borders and linking manufacturers, suppliers, and customers in different countries. As to the content of the chain, it includes services, cross-border raw materials, parts, and components. Unlike a local supply chain that operates within one country, global supply chains work on a much larger scale. GVCs account for about 70% of international trade. GVCs start with sourcing raw materials from different suppliers. Manufacturing operations may afterward take place in several countries to reduce production costs. After production, products move through distribution networks that connect factories, warehouses, and retailers worldwide.

Efficient border management reduces lead time and helps companies respond to customer demand worldwide. Several companies and service providers collaborate at each step. Maintaining strong working relationships across all partners keeps the chain efficient and reliable (Knowledge Center, 2025).

McMaster (2024) correctly notes that sometimes multilateral policy-making moves at a glacial pace, while AI will have a generalized and profound impact on trade. Therefore, there is an urgent need to build a policy architecture that reconciles trade and AI. 'There is great promise in the benefits that AI can bring. Some estimates suggest that it could raise global GDP by 7% over 10 years. However, innovation must be balanced against risks related to privacy, bias, cybersecurity and labour markets. As such, several policies have already been enacted at both an international and domestic level to navigate the costs and benefits of AI, many of which touch on trade.'

According to Krummenacher (2023) AI poses challenges to varying degrees in the world of trade policy.

Much like trade in general, AI 'will generate great economic growth but also painful labour market disruptions. Faced with the risk of worsening the digital divide by remaining inactive, policy-makers should make sure whatever solutions they arrive at contribute to creating a more sustainable and inclusive global economy.'

Trade policymakers are responding to AI, which is giving way to digitalization of the global economy, by a new wave of trade negotiations, as governments and technology firms vie to establish international rules and standards for the digital era. 'New digital trade rules include stringent intellectual property protections for source code and algorithms, and strong commitments to enable the free flow of data across borders.'

Generative Artificial Intelligence (GAI) is a subfield of AI that uses generative models to produce text, images, videos, or other forms of data. The rapid worldwide spread of GAI brings issues such as intellectual property rights, privacy violations, and cybersecurity to the fore. There are regulatory efforts by International bodies like the OECD, the UNESCO, and the G7, along with national governments. These bodies are developing principles and regulations to manage GAI's risks. Their efforts aim to balance innovation with public safety, privacy, and ethical considerations.

Governments across the world try to face AI innovations by a number of regulations, both at a national and at an international level. Mishra (2022) analyzes 'trade agreements and AI regulation as the two grow more intertwined.'

References

Cui, J. (2025). *The impact of artificial intelligence technology on cross-border trade in Southeast Asia: A meta-analytic approach.* arXiv:2503.13529 [econ.GN]. https://doi.org/10.48550/arXiv.2503.13529

Ferencz, J., López González, J., & Oliván García, I. (2022). *Artificial intelligence and international trade: Some preliminary implications.* OECD trade policy papers, no. 260. OECD publishing. https://doi.org/10.1787/13212d3e-en

Ganne, E., Locks, L., & Xu, A. (2024, November 21). *AI and international trade: Shaping and being shaped.*

Goldfarb, A., & Trefler, D. (2018). *AI and international trade.* NBER working paper series, W. P. 24254. http://www.nber.org/papers/w24254

Knowledge Center. (2025, June). *Global supply chain: What it is, importance, and challenges.* https://www.inboundlogistics.com/articles/global-supply-chain-what-it-is-importance-and-challenges/

Krummenacher, P. (2023). *International trade and artificial intelligence: Is trade policy ready for Chat GPT?* https://www.iisd.org/articles/policy-analysis/international-trade-artificial-intelligence-chatgpt

Kulesz, O. (2024). *Artificial intelligence and international cultural relations challenges and opportunities for cross-sector collaboration.* ifa (Institut für Auslandsbeziehungen e. V.).

Marr, B. (2023). The 15 biggest risks of artificial intelligence. *Forbes.* https://www.forbes.com/sites/bernardmarr/2023/06/02/the-15-biggest-risks-of-artificial-intelligence/

McMaster, P. (2024, October 9). *Why AI is the new frontier global trade must learn to cross.* World Economic Forum. https://www.weforum.org/stories/2024/10/ai-global-trade-policymaking/

Meltzer, J. P. (2018). *The impact of artificial intelligence on international trade.* https://www.brookings.edu/articles/the-impact-of-artificial-intelligence-on-international-trade/

Meltzer, J. P. (2024). The impact of foundational AI on international trade, services and supply chains in Asia. *Asian Economic Policy Review, 19*, 129–147.

Mishra, N. (2022). *Regulating artificial intelligence through digital trade agreements.* Hinrichfoundation. https://www.hinrichfoundation.com/research/wp/tech/regulating-artificial-intelligence-through-digital-trade-agreements/

O'Connor, J. (2025, April 23). *Artificial intelligence: A catalyst for de-globalization.* https://techainews.digital/2025/04/23/artificial-intelligence-a-catalyst-for-de-globalization/

Ozturk, O. (2024). The impact of AI on international trade: Opportunities and challenges by ORCID. *Qatar Economies, 12*(11), 298. https://doi.org/10.3390/economies12110298

Piao, Y. (2024). Research on the impact of artificial intelligence on international trade. Taking Alibaba international station's foreign trade AI as an example. *Transactions on Economics Business and Management Research, 9*, 163–167. https://doi.org/10.62051/5kfyd890

Rashid, A. B., & Kausik, A. K. (2024). AI revolutionizing industries worldwide: A comprehensive overview of its diverse applications. *Hybrid Advances, 7*(December), 100277. https://doi.org/10.1016/j.hybadv.2024.100277

SalesAI. (2025). *AI-powered trade automation: Enhancing efficiency in foreign trade.* https://www.saleai.io/blog/ai-powered-trade-automation-enhancing-efficiency-in-foreign-trade

Setiawan, M. A. (2025). *De-globalisation and AI.* ModernDiplomacy. https://moderndiplomacy.eu/2025/04/23/artificial-intelligence-and-the-prospect-of-de-globalization/

World Economic Forum. (2024a, September). *An analysis of generative artificial intelligence and international trade.* White paper.

World Economic Forum. (2025). *Artificial intelligence for efficiency, sustainability and inclusivity in TradeTech.* https://reports.weforum.org/docs/WEF_Artificial_Intelligence_for_Efficiency_Sustainability_and_Inclusivity_in_TradeTech_2025.pdf

Yin, Z., Wei, Q., & Lai, S. (2024). The impact of artificial intelligence technology on international trade. *Advanced International Journal of Business Entrepreneurship and SMEs, 6*(19), 153–170.

CHAPTER 5

How to Maximize the Net Effects of AI in a Globalized World

Abstract AI has emerged as a transformative influence with the capacity to reshape both our society and industries. AI devices can be employed for a number of uses (wildlife conservation, improved agriculture, healthcare diagnostics, disaster response and fighting climate-related wildfires, education, enhanced cybersecurity).

AI has been integrated in education programs at various levels, to help students for language learning and personalized learning experiences, ensuring that no one is left behind. In remote and underserved areas, AI-driven learning platforms enable access to quality education.

AI has also been recently employed to help people do common tasks faster, especially for work. One of 'the greatest advantages of AI is its ability to help people with disabilities.'

AI opens new pathways for entrepreneurship by providing tools for small businesses to compete with larger corporations.

Equitable and social issues arise with AI, as it can exacerbate inequalities if not deployed with care.

One of the primary social issues is the risk of job displacement by AI.

Keywords Maximizing the net effects of AI • Uses of AI devices • AI and the future • Number of uses of AI • AI can exacerbate inequalities • Ability to help people with disabilities • New pathways for entrepreneurship

N. Acocella, *The Economics of Globalization and Artificial Intelligence*, https://doi.org/10.1007/978-3-032-15711-9_5

The Uses of AI Devices

In an age of swift technological evolution, AI has emerged 'as a transformative influence with the capacity to reshape both our society and industries. Anchored in ethics, transparency, and accountability, the development of AI becomes pivotal, acting as the cornerstone for constructing a future that seamlessly integrates technological advancement with social responsibility.'

In the dynamic landscape of technological evolution, 'AI emerges as a pivotal force' (Bryant, 2023).

AI devices can be employed for a number of uses, such as wildlife conservation and improved agriculture, healthcare diagnostics, disaster response and fighting climate-related wildfires, education, climate change mitigation, predicting and preventing human trafficking, improving accessibility for the disabled, crop monitoring and food security, mental health support, boosted economic growth, advanced transportation, customer service excellence, scientific discovery, enhanced financial services, enhanced cybersecurity.'

Bryant (2023) notes that it is essential to consider the current influence and potential future implications of AI. AI's technology 'has the potential to automate diverse non-routine tasks across various occupations, with up to 30% of tasks in about 60% of jobs holding the potential for automation.' This almost certainly doesn't imply a jobless future, but 'underscores a pivotal shift in roles and responsibilities, emphasizing the increasing importance of adaptability in the workforce.' As Pieter den Hamer, Vice President of Research at Gartner, notes, 'every job will be impacted by AI. … Most of that will be more augmentation rather than replacing workers.' In the future AI will amplify human abilities, leading to increased innovation, productivity, and efficiency across sectors.

On the other hand, Kevin Payne and Cassidy Horton underline the need to prioritize ethical considerations in AI development, which would ensure alignment with societal values and a focus on human well-being.

Ledford (2024) notes that, despite all the doom and gloom, 'AI isn't all bad.' In fact, there can be best uses for AI in the daily life, such as 'Digital Assistants and Smart Home Devices,' which are software applications that, by using Natural Language Processing can learn voices, recognize speech pattern, and even monitor environment 'to send an alert at the sound of breaking glass or when other triggers take place.' Digital assistants' use, which is the ability to recognize words and phrases that are commonly used and to 'infer' the response you're looking for based on those words and phrases.

There can also be 'Streaming Services' to listen to music through some streaming service. AI is also used when using Netflix or Amazon Prime.

When using software applications like Adobe After Effects or Premiere Pro, Creative Work is used in a creative environment and. The company selling them 'has added AI capabilities to help creators during the editing process, specifically for video creators.'

Fitness Plans are AI-powered devices that help in realizing the need for a healthier lifestyle and have gotten much attention over the past few years.

AI has been integrated in education programs at various levels, to help students for language learning. Researchers are working on ways to integrate AI into education at all levels. AI can revolutionize education through personalized learning experiences that adapt content to meet the needs of each student, ensuring that no one is left behind. 'In remote and underserved areas, AI-driven learning platforms enable access to quality education, offering new opportunities for skill development and knowledge-sharing. For example, AI-powered platforms can create tailored learning modules based on a student's performance, preferences, and learning style.'

AI has also been recently employed to help people do common tasks faster, especially for work. An example of this are the suggestions offered by Gmail in writing something—for example, an email.

One of 'the greatest advantages of AI is its ability to help people with disabilities,' that is, 'creating accessibility.' For example, 'an image-generating AI describes the image screen readers use to help people with disabilities deciphers the images on a page. Another advancement that AI can facilitate is the diagnosis of disabilities.'

AI can help combat changes in weather patterns and facts that can be attributed to them, such as how people and animals behave, differences in our atmosphere, and increases in diseases. 'An unexpected benefit of having AI that can crunch billions of bits of data is that it can make connections faster than humans will ever be able to. Think about drug molecules that could be used to create new, more dangerous designer drugs. AI can connect the dots between those combinations, which scientists and law enforcement agencies can then use to prevent the creation of those drugs. Taking that whole idea up a notch, AI can also use that information to create safer, more effective drugs to treat diseases that have never been treatable before.'

By creating better drugs, AI can also improve our healthcare or can be used to identify disease markers in areas difficult to differentiate. In this sector, NLP enables AI systems to understand and interpret human language, which can be being used to bridge language gaps in healthcare by translating critical medical information into local languages.

Finally, AI has rapidly transformed the world, offering vast potential to revolutionize industries, economies, and society.

> One of the most compelling and positive narratives surrounding this transformative technology is its ability to be harnessed for social good. From enhancing healthcare delivery to improving disaster response, AI can be leveraged in ways that create substantial social impact, addressing many of the world's most pressing challenges. The positive uses of AI, its social impact, and how it can continue to uplift underrepresented communities can derive from the possibilities of AI: to process large amounts of data efficiently; to transform education by providing personalized learning experiences that adapt to each student's needs; to mitigate bias and inequality through responsible AI deployment, ensuring that algorithms are designed to reduce human biases and foster fair decision-making in areas like hiring and justice; to contribute significantly to climate action; to manage AI risks for ensuring that issues such as job displacement, privacy concerns, and inequality are addressed proactively, allowing AI to create equitable benefits for all.

Due to its ability to solve complex problems more efficiently and accurately than traditional methods AI can offer profound societal contributions. Apart from improving education, empowering healthcare delivery and climate, to which we have already referred, AI can address human bias, eliminating it from crucial decision-making processes, such as hiring or legal sentencing. In addition, AI can enhance public services, enabling governments to be more efficient and responsive to citizens' needs. 'One compelling example is the use of AI in predictive analytics to anticipate crime patterns, allowing law enforcement agencies to allocate resources more effectively and prevent incidents before they occur.'

Obviously, what we have said until now implies that AI can also promote economic development, having the potential to drive economic growth by improving productivity and creating new business opportunities. 'In sectors like manufacturing, AI-powered automation streamlines production processes, reduces costs, and improves product quality. By automating repetitive tasks, businesses can allocate human resources to more complex and creative work, fostering innovation and growth.' (Sigma, 2025)

At the same time, AI opens new pathways for entrepreneurship by providing tools for small businesses to compete with larger corporations. AI-powered platforms can help businesses optimize their marketing strategies, manage supply chains or offshoring, and improve customer service, leveling the playing field in the competitive global market.

AI can analyze images and videos to support efforts in disaster relief, environmental monitoring, and medical diagnostics. It can also predict future trends and outcomes in fields such as public health. Finally, AI-driven robots are used in surgery, agriculture, and disaster recovery. In agriculture, for example, AI-powered drones and robots help monitor crop health and automate tasks, ensuring food security in resource-limited regions. In post-disaster scenarios, AI-powered robots can be deployed to navigate hazardous environments and conduct search-and-rescue operations that are too dangerous for humans.

The ongoing development of these AI capabilities presents new opportunities to address some of the world's most urgent challenges. As AI continues to evolve, it has the potential to make a significant and positive impact on society.

However, AI not only carries advantages, but also introduces certain risks that need to be managed carefully, such as algorithmic bias, privacy concerns, and the potential for exacerbating inequality.

There is also a risk of privacy infringement, especially when personal data is involved, when stringent data protection measures, including encryption, anonymization, and adherence to privacy regulations like GDPR, are not introduced. Finally, a critical challenge in deploying AI for social good is maintaining transparency and accountability. 'The complex nature of AI systems can sometimes make it difficult to understand how decisions are made, leading to a lack of trust. To manage this, it's important to design AI systems that are explainable, allowing stakeholders to understand how and why decisions are reached. Moreover, organizations must implement governance frameworks that clearly define responsibility and accountability when using AI for social purposes.'

The Issues Arising from the Use of AI

We must also add that equitable and social issues arise with AI. In fact, AI can exacerbate inequalities if not deployed with care, as in the case of access to AI technologies are limited to certain groups, leaving behind underrepresented or disadvantaged communities. One of the primary social issues is the risk of job displacement, when certain jobs, particularly in sectors like manufacturing and transportation, are at risk of being replaced by AI systems. This could widen the economic divide if proper measures are not taken to retrain and reskill workers.

These examples illustrate AI's broad potential to drive meaningful social impact across various domains, proving that AI can indeed be a force for good when applied responsibly and ethically.

AI's potential to drive social good is vast, but it must be developed and applied responsibly to ensure equitable benefits.

One of the most important consideration is whether we are ready for the big ethical questions raised by AI. In particular, important are: who owns it, how its future will impact on us, its biases, transparency, privacy, safety, explainability, human oversight, trustworthiness, human-centered design, and its long-term impact on society.

Policymakers and experts are taking significant steps to understand and mitigate ethical challenges, aiming to harness AI's potential while prioritizing ethical principles (Dsouza, 2025).

To maximize AI's positive social impact, businesses, governments, and organizations must collaborate to ensure the technology is developed responsibly. Initiatives such as the 'AI for Good' Global Summit, which brings together experts to discuss how AI can be harnessed for the betterment of society, highlight the growing interest in this field.

The social impact of AI depends largely on how it is deployed. Governments must regulate AI to ensure its fair and ethical use, while businesses need to commit to developing AI solutions that benefit society at large. AI has enormous potential to address social challenges, but it is up to us to ensure that this potential is realized.

The social impact of AI for good is undeniable, but it is crucial that its deployment is guided by ethical standards. AI can make governments, businesses, and societies more resilient, responsive, and equitable, but only when developed and applied responsibly. Whether improving healthcare access, enhancing education, or safeguarding the environment, AI's potential to drive social good is vast.

The University of Cincinnati Online (2025) says that, 'at a fundamental level, AI is simply about putting human intelligence into machines. The benefits of this are numerous and far-reaching. Here are 9 amazing examples: Enhanced healthcare; Boosted economic growth; Climate change mitigation; Advanced transportation; Customer service excellence; Scientific discovery; Enhanced financial services; Improved agriculture; Enhanced cybersecurity.'

> AI tech can introduce new ways to combat cyber threats and counteract the likes of hacking attempts, ransomware, and viruses. AI programs and defenses can be set up across devices, servers, or entire networks to spot attacks in advance and take the necessary steps to mitigate their negative effects. Given the relative infancy of this industry and the very fast-evolving nature of AI, it's difficult to pin down any one dominating trend. However, with that said, there are still some noticeable patterns and themes emerging for AI in 2025 and beyond: Multimodal AI; Stronger Virtual Agents; Ethical AI Concerns and Regulations.

Fenner (2023) says that AI, with its potential to automate non-routine tasks, stands out as a transformative influence. As articulated by Berkeley Exec Ed in their recent article, the advent of the 'AI era' carries profound implications for our societies beyond technological advancements and business models. It prompts crucial questions about the evolving roles of humans as machines gain cognitive capabilities, particularly in leadership, decision-making, and strategy.

Skare and Riberio Soriano (2021) suggest that globalization is (already) a critical factor in the penetration and diffusion of digital technologies. Globalization can lower technology transfer barriers and help boost innovation and productivity. 'The self-reinforcing mechanism behind globalisation and digital technology adoption lead policymakers and practitioners to view globalization as a source of competition and as a determinant of productivity. Globalization directly affects technology adoption, which increases innovation and productivity, and therefore competitiveness and globalization (strong Granger causality).'

Kebede (2021) argues that—in order to counter the disruptive effects of technology—developing countries should build 'their human capital through careful designing of education policies and systems that embrace technological advancements' and 'should have targeted expenditure policies towards education and infrastructure.'

The benefits deriving from proposals about the use of AI are numerous. They are centered around the human life. In indicating them, we can start from personal healthcare and go to: scientific discovery, wildlife conservation, climate change mitigation, fighting climate-related wildfires, wildfire conservation, improved agriculture, social issues of AI, managing the risks of AI for social good, ensuring equitable access, disaster response, boosted economic growth, enhanced financial services, and enhanced cybersecurity. Apart from proposals for adoption of norms for regulating AI, several countries and international bodies have taken significant measures related to AI. In Europe, the AI Act has been passed and has entered into force in 2024. It says that anyone wanting to introduce AI systems or models to the EU market, will have to comply with it. In March 2024, the United Nations passed a first regulation aiming 'to bridge the digital divide between countries and promote the adoption of safe, reliable AI systems to accelerate progress towards achieving the goals of the 2030 Agenda for Sustainable Development.' The United States and the United Kingdom signed an agreement to assess and study AI-related risks, marking a major step forward in international cooperation in this field (Meroni & Zan, 2024).

To conclude this chapter, the economic impact of globalization is complex, with both positive and negative effects. 'Globalization has driven economic growth, job creation, and innovation, providing benefits to many economies and contributing to poverty reduction worldwide. However, it has also led to income inequality, job displacement, environmental degradation, and financial instability, presenting significant challenges for policymakers and businesses. Balancing the benefits and drawbacks of globalization requires concerted efforts from governments, businesses, and international organizations. To create a more equitable and sustainable global economy, it is essential to address the challenges of income inequality, environmental impact, and financial volatility. With careful management, globalization can continue to promote economic growth and interconnectedness while fostering a fair and resilient global economy for future generations.' (More, 2024).

Pavel et al. (2023) first note that 'humans organized in nation-states will have to work with another set of actors—AI-enabled machines—of equivalent or greater intelligence and, potentially, highly disruptive capabilities. In the age of geo-techno-politics, human identity and human perceptions of our roles in the world will be distinctly different; monumental scientific discoveries will emerge in ways that humans may not be able to comprehend. Consequently, the AI development path that ultimately unfolds will matter enormously for the shape and contours of the future world.'

They also give a list of what governments should do to protect humanity: (1) They should prepare for the threats posed by more-advanced AI capabilities; (2) They should also focus on strategies of resilience to mitigate potential AI threats because strategies aimed solely at denial do not work; (3) 'Governments should consider expanding their toolboxes beyond traditional regulatory techniques,' for example, by investing in the establishment of robust, publicly owned data sets for AI research or issuing challenge grants that encourage socially beneficial uses for AI; (4) Governments should continue support for innovation, either in maintaining their superiority in AI or to acquire new theoretical developments and knowledge on this matter; (5) 'Governments should work closely with leading private-sector entities to develop advanced forecasting tools, wargames, and strategic plans for dealing with what experts anticipate will be a wide variety of unexpected AI-enabled catastrophic events' (Pavel et al., 2023).

References

Bryant, K. (2023). *How AI is impacting society and shaping the future*. https://www.forbes.com/sites/kalinabryant/2023/12/13/how-ai-is-impacting-society-and-shaping-the-future/

Dsouza, J. (2025). *The importance of ethical considerations in AI development last updated: January 3*. https://zoetalentsolutions.com/ethical-considerations-in-ai-development/

Fenner, S. (2023). *Euroviews. AI has the potential to be a transformative force in the workplace*. https://www.euronews.com/next/2023/12/01/ai-has-the-potential-to-be-a-transformative-force-in-the-workplace

Kebede, M. (2021, December). *Artificial intelligence and globalization: The case of global economic outcomes for developing countries*. https://www.researchgate.net/publication/362889018_Artificial_intelligence_and_globalization_The_case_of_global_economic_outcomes_for_developing_countries_Mikyas_Kebede_Artificial_intelligence_and_globalization_The_case_of_global_economic_outcomes_for

Ledford, J. (2024, June 10). Healthcare, accessibility, and other ways AI is here to help. *Lifewire*. https://www.lifewire.com/positive-impacts-of-ai-7514777

Meroni, A., & Zan, C. (2024, August 1). *Dall'Europa al mondo: la regolamentazione dell'IA a confronto*. https://www.skilla.com/blog/dalleuropa-al-mondo-la-regolamentazione-dellia-a-confronto/
More, H. (2024, November 14). *Economic impact of globalization*. https://thefactfactor.com/facts/management/international-business/economic-impact-of-globalization/21962/
Pavel, B., Ke, I., Spirtas, M., Ryseff, J., Sabbag, L., Smith, G., Scholl, K., & Lumpkin, D. (2023). *AI and geopolitics: How might AI affect the rise and fall of nations?* RAND Corporation. https://www.rand.org/pubs/perspectives/PEA3034-1.html
Sigma. (2025, March 18). *The application of AI in manufacturing*. https://sigmatechnology.com/articles/the-application-of-ai-in-manufacturing/
Skare, M., & Riberio Soriano, D. (2021). How globalization is changing digital technology adoption: An international perspective. *Journal of Innovation & Knowledge, 6*(4), 222–233.
University of Cincinnati Online. (2025). *9 benefits of artificial intelligence (AI) in 2025*. https://online.uc.edu/blog/artificial-intelligence-ai-benefits/

CHAPTER 6

Need of a Set of Policies to Safely Leverage the Vast Potential of AI for the Benefit of Humanity

Abstract There is the need to establish a global AI regulatory watchdog as AI cannot be governed like any previous technology. The future positive or negative effects of AI will depend on what policymakers do now.

The current action of policymakers will heavily influence whether AI will cause positive advances or negative disruptions, how it will influence the structure and balance of global power.

Globalization is no longer a phenomenon driven only by the economy, but is part of a new context where political risk dominates.

Regulatory efforts to date are in their infancy and still inadequate.

At least three AI governance regimes—each with different mandates, levers, and participants—can be devised.

In June 2024, the EU adopted the world's first rules on AI.

In March 2024 the UN General Assembly adopted a landmark resolution on the promotion of safe, secure, and trustworthy AI systems.

Keywords Global AI regulation • Political risk of globalization • Inadequate regulatory efforts to date • Governance regimes • EU rules • UN General Assembly resolution

N. Acocella, *The Economics of Globalization and Artificial Intelligence*, https://doi.org/10.1007/978-3-032-15711-9_6

The Institutional Framework

Bremmer and Suleyman (2023) have noted that the UN Secretary, Antonio Guterres, called for the establishment of a global AI regulatory watchdog. In fact, AI cannot be governed like any previous technology, and it is already shifting traditional notions of geopolitical power. AI pressingly demands an original solution that agrees on basic principles for how to govern AI. The future positive or negative effects of AI will depend on what policymakers do now and the hyper-evolutionary nature of AI 'also makes solving those challenges progressively harder. That is the AI power paradox. Once released, AI models can and will be everywhere. And it will take just one malign or "breakout" model to wreak havoc. For that reason, regulating AI cannot be done in a patchwork manner. There is little use in regulating AI in some countries if it remains unregulated in others. Because AI can proliferate so easily, its governance can have no gaps.

The damage AI might do has no obvious cap, even as the incentives to build it (and the benefits of doing so) continue to grow.'

The current action of policymakers will heavily influence whether AI will cause positive advances or negative disruptions. This is more so because the 'AI developers will likely succeed in creating systems with self-improving capabilities. At the still uncertain point where AI exceeds human performance at any given task, there will be the '(admittedly speculative) peril that AGI could become self-directed, self-replicating, and self-improving beyond human control.'

Apart from this prospect, AI systems will only grow bigger, better, cheaper, and more ubiquitous and their enormous benefits become self-evident.

The development of AI will influence, and possibly shift, the structure and balance of global power, thus complicating the very political context in which it is governed.

The vast majority of countries have neither the money nor the technological know-how to compete for AI leadership. Their access to frontier AI will instead be determined by their relationships with a handful of already rich and powerful corporations and states. This dependence threatens to aggravate current geopolitical power imbalances.

Regulatory efforts to date are in their infancy and still inadequate. In fact, 'AI systems are not only infinitely easier to develop, steal, and copy than nuclear weapons; they are controlled by private companies, not governments. For global AI governance to work, it must be tailored to the specific nature of the technology, the challenges it poses, and the structure and balance of power in which it operates. But because the evolution, uses, risks, and rewards of AI are unpredictable, AI governance cannot be fully specified at the outset—or at any point in time, for that matter. It must be as innovative and evolutionary as the technology it seeks to govern, sharing some of the characteristics that make AI such a powerful force in the first place. That means starting from scratch, rethinking and rebuilding a new regulatory framework from the ground up.'

Precaution must be observed as the first and perhaps most vital principle for AI governance.

'Given the radical uncertainty about the scale and irreversibility of some of AI's potential harms, AI governance must aim to prevent these risks before they materialize rather than mitigate them after the fac

In addition to being precautionary and agile, AI governance must be inclusive, inviting the participation of all actors needed to regulate AI in practice.

Such a broadening of governance is necessary because any regulatory structure that excludes the real agents of AI power is doomed to fail. ... A single governance tool is not sufficient to address the various sources of AI risk. In practice, determining which tools are appropriate to target which risks will require developing a living and breathing taxonomy of all the possible effects AI could have—and how each can best be governed.

A minimum of three AI governance regimes, each with different mandates, levers, and participants.

The first regime would focus on fact-finding.

The world also needs a way to manage tensions between the major AI powers and prevent the proliferation of dangerous advanced AI systems. But since much of AI is already decentralized, it is a problem of the global commons rather than the preserve of two superpowers

A third AI governance regime that can react when dangerous disruptions occur.

Policymakers must build a new governance architecture to contain and harness the most formidable, and potentially defining, force of this era.'

One must take account of the new scenarios of globalization that have developed recently. In fact, it should be noted that in the last few years, the global pandemic, the disruption in supply chains, and the Russian invasion of Ukraine have been among the main factors that have strongly contributed to redrawing the map of geopolitical and economic relations at a global level, modifying both geopolitical and geoeconomic priorities.

In fact, globalization is no longer a phenomenon driven only by the economy, but is part of a new context where political risk dominates: 'Freedom is more important than free trade,' declared Jens Stoltenberg, Secretary of NATO, and with this principle the new globalization is reconfigured on the basis of new relationships between countries perceived as 'friends' and new political, economic, and military alliances as a consequence of the complex fracture that today opposes the front of Western countries to the front of the new Russian-Chinese alliance.

The Policies

Past and Current Policies

Capraro et al. (2024) underline the fact that Generative AI has the potential to both exacerbate and ameliorate existing socioeconomic inequalities. They 'provide a state-of-the-art interdisciplinary overview of the potential impacts of generative AI on (mis)information and three information-intensive domains: work, education, and healthcare,' having the goal 'to highlight how generative AI could worsen existing inequalities while illuminating how AI may help mitigate pervasive social problems. In the information domain, generative AI can democratize content creation and access but may dramatically expand the production and proliferation of misinformation. In the workplace, it can boost productivity and create new jobs, but the benefits will likely be distributed unevenly. In education, it offers personalized learning, but may widen the digital divide. In healthcare, it might improve diagnostics and accessibility, but could deepen pre-existing inequalities.' The effects will ultimately depend on the choices that we make to design and deploy the technology. Their 'responsibility extends to all sectors of society, including governance, scientific research, industry, and the public.'

On December 8, 2023, a political agreement was reached within the European Union to regulate the development of AI. In June 2024, the EU adopted the world's first rules on AI, the Artificial Intelligence Act, which will be fully applicable 24 months after entry into force. But some parts of this Act—such as the ban of AI systems posing unacceptable risks and rules on general-purpose AI systems that need to comply with transparency requirements—will be applicable sooner.

This Act is based on 'the risk levels associated with various types of applications, from a harmless spam filter to the unacceptable use of facial recognition in everyday life.' It was later revised with the addition of specific provisions on the potential of generative AI.

Some AI applications are banned[1] and some exceptions may be allowed for law enforcement purposes.

AI systems that negatively affect safety or fundamental rights are:

1. AI systems that are used in products falling under the EU's product safety legislation, such as toys, aviation, cars, medical devices, and lifts.
2. AI systems falling into specific areas that will have to be registered in an EU database and refer to, for example, management and operation of critical infrastructure; education and vocational training; employment, worker management, and access to self-employment.

All high-risk AI systems will be assessed before being put on the market.

People will have the right to complain about AI systems to designated national authorities.

High-impact general-purpose AI models that might pose systemic risk, such as the more advanced AI model GPT-4, would have to undergo thorough evaluations and any serious incidents would have to be reported to the European Commission.

Content that is either generated or modified with the help of AI—images, audio, or video files (e.g., *deepfakes*)—need to be clearly labeled as AI-generated so that users are aware when they come across such content.

The law aims to support AI innovation and start-ups in Europe, allowing companies to develop and test general-purpose AI models before public release.

That is why it requires that national authorities provide companies with a testing environment for AI that simulates conditions close to the real world. This will help small- and medium-sized enterprises (SMEs) compete in the growing EU artificial intelligence market.

The Parliament has set up a working group to oversee the implementation and enforcement of the AI Act. MEPs want to make sure that the adopted AI rules contribute to the development of the digital sector in Europe.

[1] They are: cognitive behavioral manipulation of people or specific vulnerable groups (e.g., voice-activated toys that encourage dangerous behavior in children); social scoring AI (i.e., classifying people based on behavior, socioeconomic status, or personal characteristics); biometric identification and categorization of people; real-time and remote biometric identification systems such as facial recognition in public spaces.

The group cooperates with the European Commission's EU AI office, which was set up to clarify key provisions of the Act.

The AI Act classifies AI according to its risk:

- Unacceptable risk is prohibited (e.g., social scoring systems and manipulative AI).
- Most of the text addresses high-risk AI systems, which are regulated.
- A smaller section handles limited risk AI systems, subject to lighter transparency obligations: developers and deployers must ensure that end users are aware that they are interacting with AI (chatbots and deepfakes).
- Minimal risk is unregulated (including the majority of AI applications currently available on the EU single market, such as AI enabled video games and spam filters—at least in 2021; this is changing with generative AI).

The majority of obligations fall on providers (developers) of high-risk AI systems.

In March 2024 the UN General Assembly 'adopted a landmark resolution on the promotion of "safe, secure and trustworthy" artificial intelligence (AI) systems that will also benefit sustainable development for all,' thus highlighting 'the respect, protection and promotion of human rights in the design, development, deployment and the use of AI.'

'The General Assembly also recognized AI systems' potential to accelerate and enable progress toward reaching the 17 Sustainable Development Goals.

This was the first time the Assembly adopted a resolution on regulating the emerging field. The US National Security Advisor reportedly said that the adoption would represent an "historic step forward" for the safe use of AI.

The Assembly called on all Member States and stakeholders "to refrain from or cease the use of artificial intelligence systems that are impossible to operate in compliance with international human rights law or that pose undue risks to the enjoyment of human rights" (United Nations, 2024).

Gopinath (2023) notes that we may well be at the dawn of a new technological era, that of generative artificial intelligence (AI), which could trigger radical transformations equal to those of past technology revolutions such as the printing press, electricity, the internal combustion engine and the internet. The exceptional character of generative AI is given by the speed at which it is diffusing throughout society 'and its potential to disrupt economies and even redefine what it means to be human. This is why the international community needs to agree on a set of strategic measures to ensure that AI is used for the good of humanity.'

As AI crosses borders, it is urgently necessary to establish a globally coordinated mechanism to ensure the development of this technology in a way that maximizes its enormous potential while minimizing the obvious harms to society. This will require robust and judicious measures, balancing innovation and regulation, to ensure that AI is used for the greater good.

There are various proposed legislations: by the European Union, which categorizes AI according to risk levels; the United States, which has a different approach from those of the European Union, the United Kingdom and China. 'If individual countries, or blocs of countries, adopt their own regulations or technological standards related to AI, they risk slowing the diffusion of the benefits of this technology while fueling dangerous rivalries among themselves.' Fortunately, the G7 Hiroshima Process on Generative AI, the US Executive Order on AI, and the AI Safety Summit in the United Kingdom are demonstrating a willingness to coordinate global action on AI in adopting international standards.

From the point of view of global coexistence or cooperation in digital matters, Hardman (2022) notes that governments and lawmakers are struggling 'to combine the need for global cooperation with the imperative to protect their jurisdiction from undue influence and provide economic agents with the means to compete on a global scale.' This is a concept of digital sovereignty or of strategic autonomy, to be more operative, hinting at strategic planning, and leading EU to aim at genuine digital non-alignment.

Applications of AI, in particular data-driven decision-making, concern citizens, governments, and corporations. After China, which was one of the first countries to identify AI as a key technology in which to invest heavily, many other countries and the EU have developed their own strategies. But we need to look not only to the resulting technological innovations, but also to the societal investments and applications of AI, which are so far-reaching, to be aware of the societal implications of AI applications.

New Policies

Krasodomski et al. (2024) first deal with the three epochal changes poised to reshape the US economy in coming years: an aging population driven mostly by a decline in fertility, the rise of artificial intelligence and the rewiring of the global economy. The effects of these changes will transform the lives of working people 'in ways not seen since the late 1970s, when wage inequality surged and wages at the low end stagnated or even fell.'

A similar—or even harder—problem of aging was faced over the past three decades by Japan, Germany, and South Korea. However, the economies of these countries have not grown more slowly than those of other industrialized nations 'and several of their labour-dependent sectors, including cars, machine tools and chemicals, haven't suffered.'

A broad strategy is needed for the United States, where AI must play an important role, by not only creating an automated work and sidelining workers but also creating new tasks and competencies for them.

> Evidence suggests that new technologies increase productivity much more consistently when they work with workers, enabling them to perform their jobs better and take on new, more sophisticated tasks. Most of us can become more productive and expand our range if we get better information.

AI is unlikely to become a reality by itself. It requires that AI models 'become more expert, better powered by higher-quality data, more reliable and more aligned with the existing knowledge and the information-processing capabilities of workers.' This can be done by training of workers.

Thus, aging, immigration, exploitation of AI, training, and creation of new tasks and competencies for workers can all serve to improve one another (Acemoglu, 2024).

'AI technology has become a core driving force for the development of all countries. The issue of technological hegemony—i.e. of the asymmetrical relationship between technologically developed countries and other countries by taking advantage of their dominant position in the field of technology—is one of the core issues.' This issue requires a fairer and more reasonable international AI governance system, strengthening international legal regulation, promoting multilateral cooperation and dialogue, and facilitating technology sharing and cooperation 'to enhance the technological capabilities of developing countries, and current policies still need to be changed and evolved in line with the changing international environment' (Lu, 2024).

The limits to be imposed on AI and emerging technologies are among the most pressing issues faced by society, governments, and the private sector. In fact, AI can cause many harms: it has the potential to strengthen authoritarian governance, to operate lethal autonomous weapons and form the basis for more powerful tools of societal control, surveillance, and censorship.

In public and private services there is a heightened risk of abuse of power or privacy intrusions. At the same time, AI has the potential to be enormously beneficial to humanity, but in order to harness this potential, we need to ensure that the benefits outweigh the risks, and we need some regulation. Obviously, this must be grounded in respect for human rights.

The United Nations (2023) says that 'two schools of thoughts are shaping the current development of AI regulation. The first one is risk-based only, focusing largely on self-regulation and self-assessment by AI developers … The other approach embeds human rights in AI's entire lifecycle. From beginning to end, human rights principles are included in the collection and selection of data; as well as the design, development, deployment and use of the resulting models, tools and services.'

At the international level, the United Nations can play a central role in convening key stakeholders and advising on progress. 'It may be valuable to explore the establishment of an international advisory body for particularly high-risk technologies, one that could offer perspectives on how regulatory standards could be aligned with universal human rights and rule of law frameworks. The body could publicly share the outcomes of its deliberations and offer recommendations on AI governance.'

Global AI governance wants to a better understanding and promotion of collaboration in order to create informed policies. 'It emphasizes multi-stakeholder and multi-level cooperation in managing AI's global impacts,' as AI offers exceptional benefits while carrying unintended risks, posing 'geopolitical challenges, affecting transparency, privacy and power dynamics in both democratic and non-democratic states.' 'Multilateral cooperation in global AI governance involves collaborative efforts among numerous actors to establish universally accepted norms and policies for AI. Key attributes include the following: collaborative research, union of diverse stakeholders to align policies with global ethical standards; flexible governance, adaptable to evolving AI and diverse needs; common standards for responsible AI development; harmonized regulation for unified legal and ethical standards; and universal compliance for global consistency in AI practices. An institutional framework for global AI governance should incorporate lessons from international organizations such as the International Atomic Energy Agency (IAEA) and the European Organization for Nuclear Research/Conseil Européen pour la recherche nucléaire (CERN) to guide AI's ethical development and deployment within and beyond national borders' (Niazi, 2023).

Erdélyi and Goldsmith (2022) propose the establishment of a global AI governance framework, since an adequate regulation is key to maximize the benefits and minimize the risks stemming from AI technologies. In particular, sincere international coordination is needed, supported by robust, consistent domestic, regional, and international governance arrangements. The establishment of an international AI governance framework to spearhead initiatives to create a consistent, global enabling regulatory environment, communication challenges, which they believe are underestimated barriers hindering contemporary efforts to develop AI regulatory regimes.

More cautiously, Ajami and Karimi (2023) note that AI technology 'is now in its early stages and growing fast and we should move to minimize its risks. Technological firms should not resist the demand from governments and other stakeholders to work together to mitigate and reduce the negative impact of AI tools. Rather, they should want the feedback and the input of all stakeholders and members of society in the early formative years of AI usage.'

Zakir et al. (2023), note that both the AI and the IP rights have evolved, due to fast technological advancements and corresponding legal challenges. 'As AI continues to advance, it will undoubtedly continue to test the limits of current IP frameworks, necessitating ongoing legal adaptation and reform.' Thus, 'future IP laws will need to balance the promotion of innovation with the protection of rights in a way that is ethically sound and economically viable. The need for international collaboration in developing harmonized standards and regulations will become increasingly important to address the global nature of AI technology and IP rights.'

Karakaş (2023), after having addressed possible issues posed by the AI technology, including cultural prejudices and solutions for them, provides case studies of productive AI-facilitated language exchange platforms, 'along with various AI-powered solutions that might improve learners' cross-cultural competence.'

One of the most important roots of unemployment derives from technology and, more precisely, from AI, which can lead to machines performing tasks more efficiently than men, or—more generally—from the need to reduce costs, or simply a change in work processes. Globalization of markets leads companies to seek cost-cutting solutions. In some cases, expectations of consumers change, as they often demand faster and more accurate processes.

Rapid digital transformation of traditional business models also leads to changes in the technology adopted.

Some firms have adopted proactive measures in responsible innovation, such as in the case of Google (retraining programs for workers), IBM (partnerships with universities), and Microsoft (support and professional integration projects).

It is important also to realize what the world would look like to by mid-century.

Following are some notations on that.

Based on today's innovative trends and developments, projected into the future, ten predictions have been made about what the world will be like in 2050, considering the role played by AI, even if this will be more or less pronounced for each prediction.

(1) AI and robotics for technological advances

AI will be used by humans to perform complex tasks such as medical diagnosis, smart city management and industrial production optimization. Robots will be commonly used for house cleaning, dangerous jobs and personalized services.

(2) Climate change and sustainable energy

The climate crisis will most likely have caused significant changes in the way energy is produced and consumed by 2050. Renewable energy such as solar, wind and hydrogen will be the dominant energy source in much of the world.

(3) New dynamics for work and education

Many professions that exist today will have been replaced by automation and AI. Education will have adapted to this change and will focus more on technological skills, creativity, and adaptability. Lifelong learning will become the norm, with an emphasis on continuous training and skills updates.

(4) Improved health and longer life expectancy

This will be due in particular to gene therapies and personalized treatments, prevention, and treatment of currently incurable diseases. Humans will live longer and healthier, with a higher quality of life even in old age.

(5) More pervasive globalization and connectivity

Virtual and augmented reality will provide access to immersive experiences and will change the way we work, learn, and have fun. Commercial space travel could become a reality, with a consequent start of the colonization of other planets or the construction of space habitats. Cultural differences will become increasingly thinner, thus arriving at a global society with a multiple identity.

(6) Urbanization and megacities

As the world population will continue to grow and more people will decide to live in large cities, with advanced and sustainable infrastructure, the Internet of Things (IoT) will be used in smart cities to improve the quality of life, manage resources efficiently, and reduce environmental impact.

(7) Changes in global demographics—with many developed countries dealing with an increasingly aging population, while developing countries will have a younger population—will possibly lead to mass migration and further changes in the labor market.
(8) Innovations in agriculture will be essential to feed a growing global population. These will require vertical and urban farming, genetically modified crops and sustainable agricultural practices will be commonplace. Lab-grown meat and plant-based protein alternatives could significantly reduce the environmental impact of traditional livestock farming and the future of meat production will be offered by AI.
(9) Revolution in transportation thanks to the advent of autonomous vehicles and advanced public transportation systems. Electric and hydrogen vehicles will gradually replace internal combustion engines and air travel could take place on electric and hypersonic vehicles, which make flights more sustainable and faster.
(10) Sharing economy and decentralization

The sharing of economy will be well established by 2050 and business models will favor the shared use of resources and services. Blockchain and other distributed ledger technologies will transform the way transactions, ownership, and contracts between parties are managed. Decentralization of financial, energy, and government services could become more common, increasing individual and community autonomy.[2]

Acunzo (2022) notes that 'in the last two-three years, the global pandemic, the disruption in supply chains and the Russian invasion of Ukraine are among the main factors that have strongly contributed to redrawing the map of geopolitical and economic relations at a global level, modifying both geopolitical and geo-economic priorities.'

In fact, globalization is no longer a phenomenon driven only by the economy, but is part of a new context where political risk dominates: 'Freedom is more important than free trade,' declared Jens Stoltenberg, Secretary of NATO, and with this principle the new globalization is reconfigured on the basis of new relationships between countries perceived as 'friends' and new political, economic, and military alliances as a consequence of the complex fracture that today opposes the front of Western countries to the front of the new Russian-Chinese alliance.

References

Acemoglu, D. (2024, October 17). America is sleepwalking into an economic storm. *The New York Times*.

Ajami, R. A., & Karimi, H. A. (2023). Artificial intelligence: Opportunities and challenges. *Journal of Asia-Pacific Business, 24*(2), 73–75. https://doi.org/10.1080/10599231.2023.2210239

Bremmer, I., & Suleyman, M. (2023, September/October). The AI power paradox. Can states learn to govern artificial intelligence before it's too late? *Foreign Affairs*. https://www.foreignaffairs.com/world/artificial-intelligence-power-paradox?check_logged_in=1&utm_medium=promo_email&utm_source=lo_flows&utm_campaign=article_link&utm_term=article_email&utm_content=20250601

Capraro, V., A, Lentsch, D. Acemoglu, S. Akgun, A. Akhmedova, E. Bilancini, J. F. Bonnefon, P. Brañas-Garza, L. Butera, K. M. Douglas, J. A. C. Everett, G. Gigerenzer, C. Greenhow, D. A. Hashimoto, J. Holt-Lunstad, J. Jetten, S. Johnson, W. H. Kunz, C. Longoni, P. Lunn, S. Natale, S. Paluch, I. Rahwan,

[2] Almost all these predictions have been made by medium.com › @marcwhite_72323 › predicting-the-future-is

N. Selwyn, V. Singh, S. Suri, J. Sutcliffe, J. Tomlinson, S. van der Linden, P. A. M. Van Lange, F. Wall, J. J. Van Bavel, R. Viale (2024, June 11). The impact of generative artificial intelligence on socioeconomic inequalities and policy making. *PNAS Nexus, 3*(6): 191. https://doi.org/10.1093/pnasnexus/pgae191. PMID: 38864006; PMCID: PMC11165650.

Erdélyi, O. J., & Goldsmith, J. (2022). Multidisciplinary justification for a consistent global AI governance framework. *Government Information Quarterly, 39*, 101748. https://doi.org/10.1016/j.giq.2022.101748

Gobinath, G. (2023). The Power and Perils of the "Artificial Hand": Considering AI Through the Ideas of Adam Smith, https://www.imf.org/-/media/files/publications/fandd/article/2023/december/70-72-straight-talk-final.pdf

Hardman, L. (2022). Cultural influences on artificial intelligence: Along the new silk road. In H. Werthner, E. Prem, E. A. Lee, & C. Ghezzi (Eds.), *Perspectives on digital humanism* (pp. 233–240). Springer. https://doi.org/10.1007/978-3-030-86144-5_3

Karakaş, A. (2023). Chapter 12: Breaking down barriers with artificial intelligence (AI): Cross-cultural communication in foreign language education. In *Transforming the language teaching experience in the age of AI Publisher* (Vol. 99, pp. 214–234). IGI Global. https://doi.org/10.4018/978-1-6684-9893-4.ch012

Krasodomski, A., Gwagwa, A., Jackson, B., Jones, E., King, S., Lane, M., Mantegna, M., Schneider, Th., Siminyu, K., & Tarkowski, A. (2024, June). *Artificial intelligence and the challenge for global governance.* Nine essays on achieving responsible AI, Chatham House, Research paper.

Lu, Y. (2024, December). Artificial intelligence and international law in the context of information globalization: The problem of technological hegemony as an example. *Lecture Notes in Education Psychology and Public Media, 71*(1), 75–81. https://doi.org/10.54254/2753-7048/2024.LC17962

Niazi, M. (2023). *Digital policy hub. Conceptualizing global governance of AI.* Digital Policy Hub, Center for International Governance Innovation. Working paper, chrome-extension://efaidnbmnnnibpcajpcglclefindmkaj/; https://www.cigionline.org/static/documents/DPH-paper-Niazi.pdf

United Nations. (2023, July 12). *Artificial intelligence must be grounded in human rights, says High Commissioner.* https://www.ohchr.org/en/statements-and-speeches/2023/07/artificial-intelligence-must-be-grounded-human-rights-says-high

United Nations. (2024). *General Assembly adopts landmark resolution on artificial intelligence.* https://news.un.org/en/story/2024/03/1147831

Zakir, M. H., Khan, S. H., Tanoli, K. T. K., & Sajida. (2023). The impact of artificial intelligence on intellectual property rights. *International Journal of Human and Society, 3*(4), 312–319. https://www.researchgate.net/publication/376796618_The_Impact_of_Artificial_Intelligence_on_Intellectual_Property_Rights

CHAPTER 7

Conclusions

Abstract There is a need to redefine the standard model of AI. In this model we aim to build machines able to reach the objectives stated. This can be done in several different ways, for example, by learning a policy that maximizes the expected discounted sum of rewards of the subject, who is a human. There is however a mistake in the standard model deriving from transferring to machines a definition of intelligence perfectly reasonable for humans. In fact, machines are not entitled to pursue their own objectives. A more sensible definition of AI would have machines pursuing our objectives. A new model is needed for AI development in which the machine's uncertainty about the true objective leads to qualitatively new modes of behavior that are more robust, controllable, and deferential to humans.

Keywords Redefining the standard model of AI • New models for AI development

Before concluding we must take account of the need to redefine the standard model of AI. Russell (2022) notes that in this model we aim to build machines able to reach the objectives stated. This can be done in several different ways, for example, by learning a policy that maximizes the expected discounted sum of rewards of the subject, who is a human. There

N. Acocella, *The Economics of Globalization and Artificial Intelligence*, https://doi.org/10.1007/978-3-032-15711-9_7

is however a mistake in the standard model deriving from transferring to machines a definition of intelligence perfectly reasonable for humans. In fact, machines are not entitled to pursue their own objectives. 'A more sensible definition of AI would have machines pursuing our objectives.' Russell suggests 'a new model for AI development in which the machine's uncertainty about the true objective leads to qualitatively new modes of behavior that are more robust, controllable, and deferential to humans.'

Reference

Russell, S. (2022). Artificial intelligence and the problem of control. In H. Werthner, E. Prem, E. A. Lee, & C. Ghezzi (Eds.), *Perspectives on digital humanism* (pp. 19–24). Springer. https://doi.org/10.1007/978-3-030-86144-5_3

References

Abbas Khan, M., Khan, H., Omer, M. F., Ullah, I., & Yasir, M. (2025). Impact of artificial intelligence on the global economy and technology advancements. In S. El Hajjami, K. Kaushik, & I. U. Khan (Eds.), *Artificial General Intelligence (AGI) security. Advanced technologies and societal change.* Springer. https://doi.org/10.1007/978-981-97-3222-7_7

Abduvaliev, A. (2024). The economic implications of AI on income distribution and global inequality. *Journal of New Century Innovations, 66*(1), 60–65. https://scientific-jl.org/index.php/new

Acemoglu, D. (2024, October 17). America is sleepwalking into an economic storm. *The New York Times.*

Acemoglu, D., & Restrepo, P. (2018). The race between man and machine: Implications of technology for growth, factor shares, and employment. *American Economic Review, 108*(6), 1488–1542.

Adel, A. (2022). Future of industry 5.0 in society: Human-centric solutions, challenges and prospective research areas. *J Cloud Comput (Heidelb), 11*(1):40. https://doi.org/10.1186/s13677-022-00314-5. Epub 2022 Sep 8. PMID: 36101900; PMCID: PMC9454409

Aghion, P., Antonin, C., & Bunel, S. (2019). Artificial intelligence, growth and employment: The role of policy. *Economie et Statistique / Economics and Statistics, 510-511-512*, 149–164. https://doi.org/10.24187/ecostat.2019.510t.1994

Ajami, R. A., & Karimi, H. A. (2023). Artificial intelligence: Opportunities and challenges. *Journal of Asia-Pacific Business, 24*(2), 73–75. https://doi.org/10.1080/10599231.2023.2210239

N. Acocella, *The Economics of Globalization and Artificial Intelligence*, https://doi.org/10.1007/978-3-032-15711-9

Alabdulatif, A. (2024). Technical and technological solutions towards a sustainable society and circular economy. In J. Mabrouki & A. Mourade (Eds.), *Technical and technological solutions towards a sustainable society and circular economy* (World sustainability series) (pp. 263–277). Springer. https://doi.org/10.1007/978-3-031-56292-1_21

Alyoshina, I. V. (2019). *Artificial intelligence in an age of digital globalization.* chrome-extension://efaidnbmnnnibpcajpcglclefindmkaj/ https://management-science.ru/site/public/elfinder/TEDS2019/TEDS2019-26-30-Alyoshina.pdf

Amnesty International. (2019). *Surveillance giants: How the business model of Google and Facebook threatens human rights.* file:///C:/Users/User/Downloads/POL3014042019ENGLISH.pdf

Argente, D., Moreira, S., Oberfield, E., & Venkateswaran, V. (2021, July 2). *Scalable expertise*, W. P., 4.

Asia-Pacific Economic Cooperation. (2025). *Trading with intelligence How AI shapes and is shaped by international trade.* https://mddb.apec.org/Documents/2025/MM/MRT/25_mrt_008.pdf

Autor, D. H. (2015). Why are there still so many jobs? The history and future of workplace automation. *Journal of Economic Perspectives, 29*(3): 3–30.

Avevor, M., Tawo, O. E., Akinola, O. A., Osahor, D., Awofadeju, M., & Azonuche, T. (2023). AI and technology's influence on economic inequality: A study of wealth distribution in the U.S. *World Journal of Advanced Research and Reviews, 19*(01), 1607–1617.

Barrot, J. (2024). Globalisation and higher education: Integrating generative artificial intelligence into global higher educational systems: Implications for practice, policy, and research. In J. Zajda (Ed.), *Fourth international handbook of globalisation, education and policy research* (pp. 231–250). https://doi.org/10.1007/978-3-031-67667-3_13

Baviera, A. (2025, March 26). *Intelligenza artificiale e geopolitica.* https://www.agensir.it/italia/2025/03/26/intelligenza-artificiale-e-geopolitica-berrettini-un-cattolica-tecnologia-chiave-della-competizione-globale-puo-generare-nuove-asimmetrie-di-potere/

Bendermacher, E., & Moore, M. (2024). *AI in globalization. The next mass extinction or an evolutionary leap?* Multilingual. https://multilingual.com/magazine/march-2024/ai-in-globalization/

Bibi, A. (2025, January 18). *The rise of artificial intelligence in shaping global economies.* https://moderndiplomacy.eu/2025/01/18/the-rise-of-artificial-intelligence-in-shaping-global-economies/

Bostrom, N. (2014). *Superintelligence: Paths, dangers, strategies.* Oxford University Press.

Bowles, J. (2014, July 24). *The computerisation of European jobs.* https://www.bruegel.org/blog-post/computerisation-european-jobs

Brekelmans, S., & Petropoulos, G. (2020). *Occupational change, artificial intelligence and the geography of EU labour markets, Bruegel, Stable.* https://www.jstor.org/stable/resrep50101

Bremmer, I., & Suleyman, M. (2023, September/October). The AI power paradox. Can states learn to govern artificial intelligence before it's too late? *Foreign Affairs.* https://www.foreignaffairs.com/world/artificial-intelligence-power-paradox?check_logged_in=1&utm_medium=promo_email&utm_source=lo_flows&utm_campaign=article_link&utm_term=article_email&utm_content=20250601

Bryant, K. (2023). *How AI is impacting society and shaping the future.* https://www.forbes.com/sites/kalinabryant/2023/12/13/how-ai-is-impacting-society-and-shaping-the-future/

Bughin, J., Seong, J., Manyika, J., Chui, M., & Joshi, R. (2018). *Notes from the AI frontier: Modeling the impact of AI on the world economy, September 4, Discussion paper.* https://www.mckinsey.com/featured-insights/artificial-intelligence/notes-from-the-AI-frontier-modeling-the-impact-of-ai-on-the-world-economy

Capital Economics. (2025). *AI, economies and markets – How artificial intelligence will transform the global economy.* https://www.capitaleconomics.com/ai-economies-and-markets-how-artificial-intelligence-will-transform-global-economy#table-contents

Capraro, V., A, Lentsch, D. Acemoglu, S. Akgun, A. Akhmedova, E. Bilancini, J. F. Bonnefon, P. Brañas-Garza, L. Butera, K. M. Douglas, J. A. C. Everett, G. Gigerenzer, C. Greenhow, D. A. Hashimoto, J. Holt-Lunstad, J. Jetten, S. Johnson, W. H. Kunz, C. Longoni, P. Lunn, S. Natale, S. Paluch, I. Rahwan, N. Selwyn, V. Singh, S. Suri, J. Sutcliffe, J. Tomlinson, S. van der Linden, P. A. M. Van Lange, F. Wall, J. J. Van Bavel, R. Viale (2024, June 11). The impact of generative artificial intelligence on socioeconomic inequalities and policy making. PNAS Nexus, 3(6): 191. https://doi.org/10.1093/pnasnexus/pgae191. PMID: 38864006; PMCID: PMC11165650.

Caruso, C. (2024, August 7). *The risks of artificial intelligence in weapons design.* https://hms.harvard.edu/news/risks-artificial-intelligence-weapons-design

Carvalho, J.-P. (2025, February 14). *The political-economic risks of AI.* https://ssrn.com/abstract=5137622; https://doi.org/10.2139/ssrn.5137622

Cazzaniga, M., Jaumotte, F., Li, L., Melina, G., Panton, A. J., Pizzinelli, C., Rockall, E. J., Mendes Tavares, M. (2024). *Gen-AI: Artificial intelligence and the future of work.* IMF staff discussion notes 2024/001, International Monetary Fund.

Cerutti, E. M., Pascual, A. I. G., Kido, Y., Li, L., Melina, G., Mendes Tavares, M., & Wingender, P. (2025, April 11). *The global impact of AI: Mind the gap.* IMF W. P. 76. https://doi.org/10.5089/9798229008570.001

Challoumis, C. (2024, November 15). *AI and the economy – How technology is redefining employment and income distribution*, MPRA.

Chandy, L., & Seidel, B. (2016, October 4). *Is globalization's second wave going to break? Brookings global economy and development.*

Chen, Z., Chen, C., Yang, G., He, X., Chi, X., Zeng, Z. & Chen, X. (2024, July 5). Research integrity in the era of artificial intelligence: Challenges and responses. *Medicine (Baltimore), 103*(27), e38811. https://doi.org/10.1097/MD.0000000000038811. PMID: 38968491; PMCID: PMC11224801

Cluzel-Metayer, L. (2024, avril 5). *IA: quel potentiel et quels risques dans les services publics?* Vie Publique. https://www.vie-publique.fr/parole-dexpert/293547-ia-quel-potentiel-et-quels-risques-dans-les-services-publics

Cornelli, G., Frost, J., Mishra, S. (2023, October). *Artificial intelligence, services globalisation and income inequality.* BIS working papers no 1135, Monetary and Economic Department.

Cui, J. (2025). *The impact of artificial intelligence technology on cross-border trade in Southeast Asia: A meta-analytic approach.* arXiv:2503.13529 [econ.GN]. https://doi.org/10.48550/arXiv.2503.13529

Czarnecki, T. (2024, November 5). *Do not pause advanced AI development – CONSOLIDATE AI, Sustensis, London.* https://sustensis.co.uk/

Daudin, J.-J., Li-Thiao Té, S., & Lebarbier, E. (2008). *Statistical challenges from the analysis of NGS-metagenomics experiments.* World Trade Organisation.

Dauvergne, P. (2021, February). The globalization of artificial intelligence: Consequences for the politics of environmentalism. *Globalizations, 2*(18), 285–299. https://doi.org/10.1080/14747731.2020.1785670

Development Aid. (2023, March 22). *How AI can impact developing countries: Positives and negatives.* https://www.developmentaid.org/news-stream/post/158745/how-ai-can-impact-developing-countries

Dias da Silva, A., & Weißler, M. (2025, March 21). AI adoption and employment prospects. *The ECB Blog.* https://www.ecb.europa.eu/press/blog/date/2025/html/ecb.blog20250321~6af1337b6b.en.html

Díaz-Rodríguez, N., Del Serb, J., Coeckelbergh, M., López de Prado, M., Herrera-Viedma, E., & Herrera, F. (2023). Connecting the dots in trustworthy artificial intelligence: From AI principles, ethics, and key requirements to responsible AI systems and regulation. *Information Fusion, 99*, 1–24.

Dizikes, P. (2022, November 21). Automation drives income inequality. *MIT News.* https://doi.org/10.35631/AIJBES.619012

Druzin, B., Boute, A., & Ramsden, M. (2025). Confronting catastrophic risk: The international obligation to regulate artificial intelligence. *Michigan Journal of International Law, 46*(2) https://repository.law.umich.edu/mjil/vol46/iss2/2

Dsouza, J. (2025). *The importance of ethical considerations in AI development last updated: January 3.* https://zoetalentsolutions.com/ethical-considerations-in-ai-development/

Duhienko, N. O., & Sulieimanova, A. N. (2024). Globalization and global trends: Impact of artificial intelligence on the economy. *Financial Strategies of Innovative Economic Development, 59*(3), 54–57.

Engel, C., Linhardt, L., & Schubert, M. (2025). Code is law: How COMPAS affects the way the judiciary handles the risk of recidivism. *Artificial Intelligence and Law, 33*, 383–404. https://doi.org/10.1007/s10506-024-09389-8

Erdélyi, O. J., & Goldsmith, J. (2022). Multidisciplinary justification for a consistent global AI governance framework. *Government Information Quarterly, 39*, 101748. https://doi.org/10.1016/j.giq.2022.101748

Fell, J. (2025). *Stanford just released its annual AI index report. Here's what it reveals.* World Economic Forum. https://www.weforum.org/stories/2024/04/stanford-university-ai-index-report/

Fenner, S. (2023). *Euroviews. AI has the potential to be a transformative force in the workplace.* https://www.euronews.com/next/2023/12/01/ai-has-the-potential-to-be-a-transformative-force-in-the-workplace

Ferencz, J., López González, J., & Oliván García, I. (2022). *Artificial intelligence and international trade: Some preliminary implications.* OECD trade policy papers, no. 260. OECD publishing. https://doi.org/10.1787/13212d3e-en

Fornes, G., & Altamira, M. (2023). Artificial intelligence and international business. In *Digitalization, technology and global business* (pp. 71–90). Palgrave Pivot. https://doi.org/10.1007/978-3-031-33111-4_5

Francescato, D. (2018, January 4). *Globalization, artificial intelligence, social networks and political polarization: New challenges for community psychologists, community psychology in global perspective, North America.* http://siba-ese.unisalento.it/index.php/cpgp/article/view/17684

Francisco, M. (2023). Artificial intelligence for environmental security: National, international, human and ecological perspectives. *Current Opinion in Environmental Sustainability, 61*(April), 101250. https://doi.org/10.1016/j.cosust.2022.101250

Frank, A. G., Mendes, G. H. S., Ayala, N. F., & Ghezzi, A. (2019). Servitization and industry 4.0 convergence in the digital transformation of product firms: A business model innovation perspective. *Technological Forecasting and Social Change, 141*, 341–351.

Freire, C. (2025). Is this time different? Impact of AI in output, employment and inequality across low, middle and high-income countries. *Structural Change and Economic Dynamics, 73*, 136–157.

Frey, C., & Osborne, M. (2013). *The future of employment: How susceptible are jobs to computerisation?* Working paper, University of Oxford.

Furman, J., & Seamans, R. (2019). AI and the economy. *Innovation Policy and the Economy, 19*, 161–191. https://doi.org/10.1086/699936

Gale, R., & Null, G. (2025, May 31). *The coming artificial intelligence crisis: Power without oversight, global research.* https://www.globalresearch.ca/coming-artificial-intelligence-crisis/5888723

Ganne, E., Locks, L., & Xu, A. (2024, November 21). *AI and international trade: Shaping and being shaped.*

García, S. (2024, June 4). *AI and the globalization of labor markets.* https://www.futureforwork.com/en/ai-and-the-globalization-of-labor-markets/

Georgieff, A., & Hyee, R. (2022). Artificial intelligence and employment: New cross-country evidence. *Frontiers in Artificial Intelligence, 5*, 832736. https://doi.org/10.3389/frai.2022.832736

Georgieva, K. (2024, January 14). AI will transform the global economy. Let's make sure it benefits humanity. *IMF Blog.* https://www.imf.org/en/Blogs/Articles/2024/01/14/ai-will-transform-the-global-economy-lets-make-sure-it-benefits-humanity

Gerlich, M. (2024). Brace for impact: Facing the AI revolution and geopolitical shifts in a future societal scenario for 2025–2040. *Societies, 14*(9), 180. https://doi.org/10.3390/soc14090180

Ghosh, D., Ghosh, R., Chowdhury, S. R., & Ganguly, B. (2025). AI-exposure and labour market: A systematic literature review on estimations, validations, and perceptions. *Management Review Quarterly, 2025*(75), 677–704. https://doi.org/10.1007/s11301-023-00393-x

Giattino, C., Mathieu, E., Samborska, V., & Roser, M. (2023). *Artificial intelligence.* Published online at OurWorldinData.org. https://ourworldindata.org/artificial-intelligence

Global Transactions. (2020, January 16). *The impact of AI on global expansion.* https://www.globalization-partners.com/blog/the-impact-of-ai-on-global-expansion/

Gobinath, G. (2023). The Power and Perils of the "Artificial Hand": Considering AI Through the Ideas of Adam Smith, https://www.imf.org/-/media/files/publications/fandd/article/2023/december/70-72-straight-talk-final.pdf

Goldfarb, A., & Trefler, D. (2018). *AI and international trade.* NBER working paper series, W. P. 24254. http://www.nber.org/papers/w24254

Goyal, A., & Aneja, R. (2020). Artificial intelligence and income inequality: Do technological changes and worker's position matter? *Journal of Public Affairs*, 02 September, https://doi.org/10.1002/pa.2326

Greenbaum, L., Long, F., & Shirley, W. (2023, December 14). *The generative world order: AI, geopolitics, and power.* https://www.goldmansachs.com/insights/articles/the-generative-world-order-ai-geopolitics-and-power

Gries, Th., & Naudé, W. (2020). Artificial Intelligence, income distribution and economic growth, GLO Discussion Paper Series 632, Global Labor Organization (GLO).

Guarascio, D., & Reljic, J. (2025). AI and employment in Europe. *Economics Letters, 247*(February), 112183. https://doi.org/10.1016/j.econlet.2025.112183

Guliyev, H. (2023). Artificial intelligence and unemployment in high-tech developed countries: New insights from dynamic panel data model. *Research in Globalization, 7*, 100140. www.sciencedirect.com/journal/research-in-globalization

Guryanova, A. V., Shestakov, A. A., & Tikhonov, V. (2021). Digital globalization as a result of the modern economic and technological development. In S. I. Ashmarina, V. V. Mantulenko, M. I. Inozemtsev, & E. L. Sidorenko (Eds.), *Global challenges and prospects of the modern economic development* (European proceedings of social and behavioural sciences) (Vol. 106, pp. 787–792). European Publisher. https://doi.org/10.15405/epsbs.2021.04.02.94

Hagerty, A., & Rubinov, I. (2019). *Global AI ethics: A review of the social impacts and ethical implications of artificial intelligence.* https://doi.org/10.48550/arXiv.1907.07892

Hardman, L. (2022). Cultural influences on artificial intelligence: Along the new silk road. In H. Werthner, E. Prem, E. A. Lee, & C. Ghezzi (Eds.), *Perspectives on digital humanism* (pp. 233–240). Springer. https://doi.org/10.1007/978-3-030-86144-5_3

Held, D., McGrew, A. G., Goldblatt, D., & Perraton, J. (1999). *Global transformations: Politics, economics, and culture.* Stanford University Press.

How to use AI in Foreign sales. https://www.chiterion.com/how-to-use-ai-in-foreign-sales

Ibrahim, I. A., Abdurrahman, I. A., & Baballe, M. A. (2025). Navigating the challenges of industry 5.0: How artificial intelligence is revolutionising the future of work. *Global Journal of Research in Engineering & Computer Sciences, 5*(3), 59–66. ISSN: 2583-2727. https://www.researchgate.net/publication/392129633

Ilzetzki, E., & Suryaansh, J. (2023, June 20). *The impact of artificial intelligence on growth and employment.* https://cepr.org/voxeu/columns/impact-artificial-intelligence-growth-and-employment

International Trade Council. (2023). *Artificial intelligence and the future of international trade.* https://tradecouncil.org/wp-content/uploads/2024/10/artificial-intelligence-and-the-future-of-international-trade.pdf

Iqbal, M. S., & Fikri, S. M. (2025). Impact of globalisation, AI adoption, and FinTech integration on banking sector performance and customer satisfaction in post-COVID Pakistan. *The Pakistan Development Review, 64*(1), 1–23.

Jacks, D. S., & Tang, J. P. (2018). *Trade and immigration, 1870–2010.* NBER W. P, 25010. http://www.nber.org/papers/w25010

Jones, E. (2023). Digital disruption: Artificial Intelligence and international trade policy. *Oxford Review of Economic Policy, 39*(1), 70–84. https://doi.org/10.1093/oxrep/grac049

Kanungo, A. (2023). *The real environmental impact of AI.* https://earth.org/the-green-dilemma-can-ai-fulfil-its-potential-without-harming-the-environment/

Karakaş, A. (2023). Chapter 12: Breaking down barriers with artificial intelligence (AI): Cross-cultural communication in foreign language education. In *Transforming the language teaching experience in the age of AI Publisher* (Vol. 99, pp. 214–234). IGI Global. https://doi.org/10.4018/978-1-6684-9893-4.ch012

Kebede, M. (2021, December). *Artificial intelligence and globalization: The case of global economic outcomes for developing countries.* https://www.researchgate.net/publication/362889018_Artificial_intelligence_and_globalization_The_case_of_global_economic_outcomes_for_developing_countries_Mikyas_Kebede_Artificial_intelligence_and_globalization_The_case_of_global_economic_outcomes_for

Khan, M. W., Destek, M. A., & Khan, Z. (2025). Income inequality and artificial intelligence: Globalization and age dependency for developed countries. *Social Indicators Research: An International and Interdisciplinary Journal for Quality-of-Life Measurement, 176*(3), 1207–1233.

Klasing, M. J., & Milionis, P. (2014). Quantifying the evolution of world trade, 1870–1949. *Journal of International Economics, 92*(1), 185–197. Available at SSRN: https://ssrn.com/abstract=2413883

Knowledge Center. (2025, June). *Global supply chain: What it is, importance, and challenges.* https://www.inboundlogistics.com/articles/global-supply-chain-what-it-is-importance-and-challenges/

Knudsen, J. E., Ghaffar, U., Ma, R., & Hung, A. J. (2024). Clinical applications of artificial intelligence in robotic surgery. *Journal of Robotic Surgery, 18*(1), 102. https://doi.org/10.1007/s11701-024-01867-0

Korinek, A., & Stiglitz, J. (2025, May 5). *Steering technological progress.* INET W. P. No. 232.

Krasodomski, A., Gwagwa, A., Jackson, B., Jones, E., King, S., Lane, M., Mantegna, M., Schneider, Th., Siminyu, K., & Tarkowski, A. (2024, June). *Artificial intelligence and the challenge for global governance.* Nine essays on achieving responsible AI, Chatham House, Research paper.

Krummenacher, P. (2023). *International trade and artificial intelligence: Is trade policy ready for Chat GPT?* https://www.iisd.org/articles/policy-analysis/international-trade-artificial-intelligence-chatgpt

Kulesz, O. (2024). *Artificial intelligence and international cultural relations challenges and opportunities for cross-sector collaboration.* ifa (Institut für Auslandsbeziehungen e. V.).

Kumar, D., Jain, R., & Deb, V. (2018). Artificial Intelligence. Creating automated insights for customer relationship management, January, https://doi.org/10.1109/CONFLUENCE.2018.8442900, 8th International Conference on Cloud Computing, Data Science & Engineering (Confluence).

Lanzi, D. (2025, January). *Artificial intelligence, development, and stratification economics*. https://doi.org/10.13140/RG.2.2.20639.06569. https://www.researchgate.net/publication/388449295_Artificial_Intelligence_Development_and_Stratification_Economics

Ledford, J. (2024, June 10). Healthcare, accessibility, and other ways AI is here to help. *Lifewire*. https://www.lifewire.com/positive-impacts-of-ai-7514777

Levitt, T. (1983, May). The globalization of markets. *Harvard Business Review*. https://hbr.org/1983/05/the-globalization-of-markets

Liang, Y. (2024, March, 27). The impact of artificial intelligence on employment and income distribution. *Journal of Education Humanities and Social Sciences*, 166–171. https://doi.org/10.54097/2a7a8830

Liu, F., & Liang, C. (2025). Analyzing wealth distribution effects of artificial intelligence: A dynamic stochastic general equilibrium approach. *Heliyon*, 11.

Lowitzsch, J., & Magalhães, R. (2025). Automation, artificial intelligence and capital concentration – A race for the machine. *International Review of Applied Economics, 39*(2–3), 197–215.

Lu, Y. (2024, December). Artificial intelligence and international law in the context of information globalization: The problem of technological hegemony as an example. *Lecture Notes in Education Psychology and Public Media, 71*(1), 75–81. https://doi.org/10.54254/2753-7048/2024.LC17962

Lumenalta. (2024, September 5). *Positive impacts of AI for good*. https://lumenalta.com/insights/the-positive-impact-of-ai-for-good

Magistro, B., Borwein, S., Michael Alvarez, R., Bonikowski, B., & Loewen, P. J. (2025). Attitudes toward artificial intelligence (AI) and globalization: Common microfoundations and political implications. *American Journal of Political Science*, 1–18. https://doi.org/10.1111/ajps.12959

Maietta, C. (2020, January 31). *Se lo scrittore è un algoritmo: L'AI per la letteratura*. https://www.ai4business.it/intelligenza-artificiale/se-lo-scrittore-e-un-algoritmo-lai-per-la-letteratura/

Marchand, A., & Sotelo, J. (2025). *Artificial intelligence for efficiency, sustainability and inclusivity in tradetech*.

Marr, B. (2023). The 15 biggest risks of artificial intelligence. *Forbes*. https://www.forbes.com/sites/bernardmarr/2023/06/02/the-15-biggest-risks-of-artificial-intelligence/

Matyushok, V., Krasavina, V., Berezin, A., & Sendra García, J. (2021). The global economy in technological transformation conditions: A review of modern trends. *Economic Research-Ekonomska Istraživanja, 34*(1), 1471–1497. https://doi.org/10.1080/1331677X.2020.1844030

McKinsey & Company Global Institute. (2023, June). *The economic potential of generative AI. The next productivity frontier.* https://www.mckinsey.com/~/media/mckinsey/business%20functions/mckinsey%20digital/our%20insights/the%20economic%20potential%20of%20generative%20ai%20the%20next%20productivity%20frontier/the-economic-potential-of-generative-ai-the-next-productivity-frontier.pdf

McLaughlin, M. (2023). Regulating artificial intelligence in international investment law. *Journal of World Investment & Trade, 24*, 256–300.

McMaster, P. (2024, October 9). *Why AI is the new frontier global trade must learn to cross.* World Economic Forum. https://www.weforum.org/stories/2024/10/ai-global-trade-policymaking/

Meeting the AI moment; World Economic Forum. https://reports.weforum.org/docs/WEF_Artificial_Intelligence_for_Efficiency_Sustainability_and_Inclusivity_in_TradeTech_2025.pdf

Melitz, M. (2003). The impact of trade on aggregate industry productivity and intra-industry reallocations. *Econometrica, 71*(6), 16951725.

Meltzer, J. P. (2018). *The impact of artificial intelligence on international trade.* https://www.brookings.edu/articles/the-impact-of-artificial-intelligence-on-international-trade/

Meltzer, J. P. (2024). The impact of foundational AI on international trade, services and supply chains in Asia. *Asian Economic Policy Review, 19*, 129–147.

Menzies, J., Sabert, B., Hassan, R., & Kofi Mensah, P. (2024). Artificial intelligence for international business: Its use, challenges, and suggestions for future research and practice. *Thunderbird International Business Review.* https://doi.org/10.1002/tie.22370

Meroni, A., & Zan, C. (2024, August 1). *Dall'Europa al mondo: la regolamentazione dell'IA a confronto.* https://www.skilla.com/blog/dalleuropa-al-mondo-la-regolamentazione-dellia-a-confronto/

Miguelañez, C. (2025, January 11). *LLM prompt engineering FAQ: Exper, latitude.*https://latitude-blog.ghost.io/blog/llm-prompt-engineering-faq-expert-answers-to-common-questions/

Mishra, N. (2022). *Regulating artificial intelligence through digital trade agreements.* Hinrichfoundation. https://www.hinrichfoundation.com/research/wp/tech/regulating-artificial-intelligence-through-digital-trade-agreements/

MIT Technology Review Insights. (2023). *The great acceleration: CIO perspectives on generative AI.* https://www.technologyreview.com/2023/07/18/1076423/the-great-acceleration-cio-perspectives-on-generative-ai/

Monostori, L. (2014). Artificial intelligence. In L. Laperrière & G. Reinhart (Eds.), *CIRP encyclopedia of production engineering.* Springer. https://doi.org/10.1007/978-3-642-20617-7_16703

More, H. (2024, November 14). *Economic impact of globalization.* https://thefactfactor.com/facts/management/international-business/economic-impact-of-globalization/21962/

Niazi, M. (2023). *Digital policy hub. Conceptualizing global governance of AI*. Digital Policy Hub, Center for International Governance Innovation. Working paper, chrome-extension://efaidnbmnnnibpcajpcglclefindmkaj/; https://www.cigionline.org/static/documents/DPH-paper-Niazi.pdf

Nordregio. (n.d.). *The three waves of globalisation*. https://archive.nordregio.se/en/Metameny/About-Nordregio/Journal-of-Nordregio/2008/Journal-of-Nordregio-no-1-2008/The-Three-Waves-of-Globalisation/index.html

O'Connor, J. (2025, April 23). *Artificial intelligence: A catalyst for de-globalization*. https://techainews.digital/2025/04/23/artificial-intelligence-a-catalyst-for-de-globalization/

Ozturk, O. (2024). The impact of AI on international trade: Opportunities and challenges by ORCID. *Qatar Economies, 12*(11), 298. https://doi.org/10.3390/economies12110298

Pavel, B., Ke, I., Spirtas, M., Ryseff, J., Sabbag, L., Smith, G., Scholl, K., & Lumpkin, D. (2023). *AI and geopolitics: How might AI affect the rise and fall of nations?* RAND Corporation. https://www.rand.org/pubs/perspectives/PEA3034-1.html

Pedamkar, P. (2023). *Statistics for machine learning*. EDUCBA. https://www.educba.com/statistics-for-machine-learning/

Perlant, C. (2025). Modéliser les épidémies à l'ère de l'intelligence artificielle. *Médecine de Catastrophe Urgences Collectives, 9*(2), 93–95.

Pew Research Center. (2023, July 21). *What shares of workers are most exposed to AI in their jobs?* https://www.pewresearch.org/social-trends/2023/07/26/which-u-s-workers-are-more-exposed-to-ai-on-their-jobs/st_2023-07-26_ai-and-jobs_0-01-png/

Piao, Y. (2024). Research on the impact of artificial intelligence on international trade. Taking Alibaba international station's foreign trade AI as an example. *Transactions on Economics Business and Management Research, 9*, 163–167. https://doi.org/10.62051/5kfyd890

Provenzani, F. (2024). *What the world will be like in 2050 according to artificial intelligence, August 18, – Predicting the future is always a challenge, but based on current trends and expectations on technological, social and economic developments*. https://en.money.it/What-the-world-will-be-like-in-2050-according-to-AI

PWC. (n.d.). *Sizing the prize. What's the real value of AI for your business and how can you capitalise?* chrome-extension://efaidnbmnnnibpcajpcglclefindmkaj/, https://www.pwc.com/gx/en/issues/analytics/assets/pwc-ai-analysis-sizing-the-prize-report.pdf

Rana, D. (2022, December 13). The impact of AI on global expansion. *Indian Journal of Law and Legal Research, IV*(VI), 1–21.

Rashid, A. B., & Kausik, A. K. (2024). AI revolutionizing industries worldwide: A comprehensive overview of its diverse applications. *Hybrid Advances, 7*(December), 100277. https://doi.org/10.1016/j.hybadv.2024.100277

Ratten, V. (2024). Artificial intelligence, digital trends and globalization: Future research trends. *FIIB Business Review, 13*(3), 286–293. https://doi.org/10.1177/23197145231222774

Rui, Z., & Bhaumik, A. (2023). A new phase of global streams artificial intelligence and cyber security. *International Journal for Multidisciplinary Research Digital Globalization, 5*(4), 1–11.

Russell, S. (2022). Artificial intelligence and the problem of control. In H. Werthner, E. Prem, E. A. Lee, & C. Ghezzi (Eds.), *Perspectives on digital humanism* (pp. 19–24). Springer. https://doi.org/10.1007/978-3-030-86144-5_3

Saeed, R. (2023). *The future of AI. Unleashing intelligence for limitless outcomes.* https://www.linkedin.com/pulse/future-ai-unleashing-potential-artificial-rabia-saeed

Saeed, M., & Sofi, F. (2025, April). Impact of globalisation, AI adoption, and Fintech integration on banking sector performance and customer satisfaction in post-covid Pakistan. *The Pakistan Development Review.* https://doi.org/10.30541/v64i1pp.1-23

SalesAI. (2025). *AI-powered trade automation: Enhancing efficiency in foreign trade.* https://www.saleai.io/blog/ai-powered-trade-automation-enhancing-efficiency-in-foreign-trade

Schellekens, Ph., & Skilling, D. (2024, October 17). *Three reasons why AI may widen global inequality.* Center for Global Development. https://www.cgdev.org/blog/three-reasons-why-ai-may-widen-global-inequality

Schwab, K. (2017). *The fourth industrial revolution.* Crown Business.

Schwalbe, N., & Wahl, B. (2020). Artificial intelligence and the future of global health. *The Lancet, 395*, 1579–1586. chrome-extension://efaidnbmnnnibpcajpcglclefindmkaj/ https://www.thelancet.com/action/showPdf?pii=S0140-6736%2820%2930226-9

Sethi, K. C. (2025, March 15). *Come l'intelligenza artificiale e la globalizzazione stanno ridefinendo la diversità letteraria.* com.unica. https://www.agenziacomunica.net/2025/02/15/come-lintelligenza-artificiale-e-la-globalizzazione-stanno-ridefinendo-la-diversita-letteraria/

Setiawan, M. A. (2025). *De-globalisation and AI.* ModernDiplomacy. https://moderndiplomacy.eu/2025/04/23/artificial-intelligence-and-the-prospect-of-de-globalization/

Shanmugasundaram, M., & Tamilarasu, A. (2023, November 24). The impact of digital technology, social media, and artificial intelligence on cognitive functions: A review. *Frontiers in Cognition,* Sec. Learning and Cognitive Development, *2*. https://doi.org/10.3389/fcogn.2023.1203077

Shen, Y., & Zhang, X. (2024). The impact of artificial intelligence on employment. The role of virtual agglomeration. *Humanities and Social Sciences Communications, 11*, 122. https://doi.org/10.1057/s41599-024-02647-9

Sholler, D., & MacInnes, I. (2024). AI and income inequality: The danger of exacerbating existing trends toward polarization in the US workforce. In M. Garcia-Murillo, I. MacInnes, & A. Renda (Eds.), *Chapter 17 of Handbook of artificial intelligence at work* (pp. 338–355). Elgar. https://doi.org/10.4337/9781800889972.000

Sichach, M. (2023, September 22). *Technology and globalisation: How social media (narrow artificial intelligence) algorithms and large language models by internet companies have replaced the main stream media as agenda setters for the global culture.* https://ssrn.com/abstract=4580284; https://doi.org/10.2139/ssrn.4580284

Sigma. (2025, March 18). *The application of AI in manufacturing.* https://sigmatechnology.com/articles/the-application-of-ai-in-manufacturing/

Skare, M., Gavurova, B., & Blažević Burić, S. (2024). Artificial intelligence and wealth inequality: A comprehensive empirical exploration of socioeconomic implications. *Technology in Society, 79*, 102719.

Skare, M., & Riberio Soriano, D. (2021). How globalization is changing digital technology adoption: An international perspective. *Journal of Innovation & Knowledge, 6*(4), 222–233.

Smith, B. (2023, February 2). *Meeting the AI moment: Advancing the future through responsible AI.* https://aiandyou.org/news/meeting_the_ai_moment/

Sociology Institute. (2023). *Sociology-of-development.* https://sociology.institute/sociology-of-development/

Solos, W. K., & Leonard, J. (2022). On the impact of artificial intelligence on economy. *Science Insights, 41*(1), 501–560.

Spence, M. (2024). *AI's promise for the global economy.* https://www.imf.org/en/Publications/fandd/issues/2024/09/AIs-promise-for-the-global-economy-Michael-Spence#:~:text=With%20policy%20support,aggressively%20but%20wisely

Statistics Canada. (2019). *Canada at a glance.* chrome-extension://efaidnbmnnnibpcajpcglclefindmkaj/ https://www150.statcan.gc.ca/n1/en/pub/12-581-x/12-581-x2019001-eng.pdf?st=b2VnDkJg

Stiglitz, J. E., & Korinek, A. (2025, May 22). The future of inequality: Artificial intelligence, worker-replacing technological progress and income distribution. In *The origins of inequality* (online ed.). Oxford Academic. https://doi.org/10.1093/oso/9780198799580.003.0019

Team GP. (2020, gennaio 16). *L'impatto dell'intelligenza artificiale sull'espansione globale.* https://www.globalization-partners.com/it/blog/the-impact-of-ai-on-global-expansion/

Thunderbird. (2024, October 25). *Global AI and the future of work.* https://thunderbird.asu.edu/thought-leadership/insights/global-ai-future-of-work

United Nations. (2023, July 12). *Artificial intelligence must be grounded in human rights, says High Commissioner.* https://www.ohchr.org/en/statements-and-speeches/2023/07/artificial-intelligence-must-be-grounded-human-rights-says-high

United Nations. (2024). *General Assembly adopts landmark resolution on artificial intelligence.* https://news.un.org/en/story/2024/03/1147831

United Nations. (2025, May 20). *AI threatens one in four jobs – But transformation, not replacement, is the real risk.* https://news.un.org/en/story/2025/05/1163486

United Nations Regional Information Centre for Western Europe. (2025, April 30). *Artificial intelligence and the future of work: Will AI replace our jobs?* https://unric.org/en/artificial-intelligence-and-the-future-of-work-will-ai-replace-our-jobs/

University of Berkeley. (n.d.). *The future of work & leadership in the age of AI.* https://executive.berkeley.edu/thought-leadership/blog/future-work-leadership-age-ai

University of Cincinnati Online. (2025). *9 benefits of artificial intelligence (AI) in 2025.* https://online.uc.edu/blog/artificial-intelligence-ai-benefits/

Vesely, S., & Amaris, G. (2025). AI-driven income inequality and preferences for redistribution. *Economic Analysis and Policy, Qeios.* https://doi.org/10.32388/7HWUZ2

Vezzoli, M. (2024, February 2). *L'impatto dell'AI nella sfida della globalizzazione.* https://tinnovamag.com/limpatto-dellai-nella-sfida-della-globalizzazione/

Wagner, D. (2018). *How artificial intelligence is changing the global economy, science & technology: Innovation, governance, economics, technology.* https://ourworld.unu.edu/en/how-ai-is-changing-the-global-economy

Wang, C., & Jiao, D. (2025). Impact of artificial intelligence on the labor income distribution: Labor substitution or production upgrading? *Finance Research Letters, 73*(C) Elsevier.

Wang, Q., Sun, T., & Li, R. (2023). Does artificial intelligence (AI) reduce ecological footprint? The role of globalization. *Environmental Science and Pollution Research, 30*, 123948–123965. https://doi.org/10.1007/s11356-023-31076-5

Weber, S. (2019). *Bloc by Bloc. How to build a global enterprise for the new regional order.* Harvard University Press.

Weber, S., & Stanton, Ch. (2019). *The world isn't ready for AI to upend the global economy.* https://carnegieendowment.org/posts/2019/10/the-world-isnt-ready-for-ai-to-upend-the-global-economy?lang=en

West, D. M. (2018, October 4). *What is artificial intelligence?* https://www.brookings.edu/articles/what-is-artificial-intelligence/

Wodecki, A. (2019). *Artificial intelligence in value creation. Improving competitive advantage.* Palgrave Macmillan.

World Bank. (2020). *Artificial intelligence in the public sector. Maximizing opportunities, managing risks.* chrome-extension://efaidnbmnnnibpcajpcglclefindmkaj/, https://documents1.worldbank.org/curated/en/809611616042736565/pdf/Artificial-Intelligence-in-the-Public-Sector-Maximizing-Opportunities-Managing-Risks.pdf

World Economic Forum. (2024a, September). *An analysis of generative artificial intelligence and international trade.* White paper.

World Economic Forum. (2024b, September). ChatWTO: An analysis of generative artificial intelligence and international trade. White paper. https://www3.weforum.org/docs/WEF_An_Analysis_of_Generative_Artificial_Intelligence_and_International_Trade_2024.pdf

World Economic Forum. (2025). *Artificial intelligence for efficiency, sustainability and inclusivity in TradeTech.* https://reports.weforum.org/docs/WEF_Artificial_Intelligence_for_Efficiency_Sustainability_and_Inclusivity_in_TradeTech_2025.pdf

World Trade Organization. (2008). *World trade report 2008. Trade in a globalizing world.* https://www.wto-ilibrary.org/content/books/9789287044952/read

Yin, Z., Wei, Q., & Lai, S. (2024). The impact of artificial intelligence technology on international trade. *Advanced International Journal of Business Entrepreneurship and SMEs, 6*(19), 153–170.

Yudkowsky, E. (2023, March 29). Pausing AI developments isn't enough. We need to shut it all down. *Time.* https://time.com/6266923/ai-eliezer-yudkowsky-open-letter-not-enough/

Zakir, M. H., Khan, S. H., Tanoli, K. T. K., & Sajida. (2023). The impact of artificial intelligence on intellectual property rights. *International Journal of Human and Society, 3*(4), 312–319. https://www.researchgate.net/publication/376796618_The_Impact_of_Artificial_Intelligence_on_Intellectual_Property_Rights

Zhu, K. (2025, April 27). *Technology visualizing U.S. vs. Chinese AI model performance.* https://www.visualcapitalist.com/visualizing-u-s-vs-chinese-ai-model-performance/

Index[1]

[1] Note: Page numbers followed by 'n' refer to notes.

N. Acocella, *The Economics of Globalization and Artificial Intelligence*, https://doi.org/10.1007/978-3-032-15711-9

FSC
www.fsc.org
MIX
Papier | Fördert
gute Waldnutzung
FSC® C083411

Kolibri 360 GmbH
Ferdinand-Jühlke-Straße 7
99095 Erfurt, Deutschland
produktsicherheit@kolibri360.de